tarrygray

SPHERE

Andrew Arden is
Guides. He is a barris...
on housing law in Britain. He is also the editor of the *Encyclopaedia of Housing Law* and the *Housing Law Reports*. He is the author of three novels, one of which, *No Certain Roof*, is about landlord and tenant. He has written two other Sphere Guides – *The Homeless Persons Handbook* and *The Public Tenants Handbook*.

SPHERE RIGHTS GUIDES
Series Editor: Andrew Arden

THE PRIVATE TENANTS HANDBOOK

ANDREW ARDEN

SPHERE REFERENCE

SPHERE BOOKS LTD

First published in Great Britain
by Allison and Busby 1985
This revised edition published
by Sphere Books Limited 1989
Copyright © Andrew Arden 1985, 1989

ISBN 0-7474-0223-X

Typeset in Plantin by Leaper & Gard Ltd, Bristol, England
Printed and bound in Great Britain by
The Guernsey Press

Sphere Books Ltd
A Division of
Macdonald & Co (Publishers) Ltd
27 Wrights Lane
London W8 5TZ
A Maxwell Pergamon Publishing Corporation plc

Contents

5. Security of Tenure   102

8. Controls on Rents   153

9. Repairs, Improvements and Alterations   173

REPAIRS

Publisher's Note

The law on housing can change at short notice. This book
describes the law as at May 1989. You should always check
if what it says is still correct.

Introduction

This is one of a number of books dealing with the rights of:

Private Tenants. Weekly, monthly or other periodic tenants, and tenants with leases of twenty-one years or less, together with lesser rights of occupation known as licences, in houses, flats or rooms, where the landlord is a private individual or company, or some other body whose tenants are not public tenants, and who does not otherwise fall within one of the following classes.

Public Tenants. Weekly, monthly or other periodic tenants, and tenants with leases of twenty-one years or less, together with lesser rights of occupation known as licences, in houses, flats or rooms, where the landlord is a local authority, registered housing association or trust, or a development corporation or housing action trust, and who does not fall within one of the following classes.

Owner Occupiers. Those who – with or without a mortgage – have a freehold interest in a house or flat, or a lease of more than twenty-one years.

Occupiers of Mobile Homes. Those living in caravans, houseboats or other moveable structures, whether they own those structures or rent them from other people.

Tied Occupiers. Those who have accommodation – in houses, flats or rooms – from their employers, or otherwise on account of their employment.

Homeless Persons. Those who do not have a home in which they have a right to live together with those members of their families they would reasonably be expected to live with.

An additional volume in this series will deal with *Housing Benefit* for all of the above.

These books do not cover the rights of individuals who have been living somewhere as husband and wife (whether or not legally married) on a domestic breakdown: see the *Divorce Handbook* in this series. This book does not deal with the rights of tenants against each other, for example neighbouring tenants.

The law in Scotland and in Northern Ireland is different from the law in England and Wales which is described in this book; many of the details of the law are different, there are procedural differences, and in some cases there are actual differences in rights. However, much of the information contained in this book concerns rights which Parliament has given to tenants and other occupiers, and as a general rule when Parliament gives rights to occupiers in England and Wales it will seek to give the same or similar rights to occupiers in Scotland, and sometimes also in Northern Ireland.

    As an outline of what may well be available, this book may therefore still be of use to those in Scotland and Northern Ireland, although they should always be careful to check the position independently. Useful places to check are:

Shelter (Scotland),
65 Cockburn Street,
Edinburgh EH1 1BU.
Tel: Edinburgh (031) 226 6347

Shelter (Northern Ireland),
2b John Street,
Omagh, Co. Tyrone.
Tel: Omagh (0662) 44985

The law on housing rights changes frequently. This book describes the law as at 31 May 1989. You should always check if what it says is still correct.

This book is an outline of what rights are likely to be available to you, as a private tenant. For a number of reasons, it cannot tell you in precise detail the full extent of your rights in every situation. For one thing, what your rights are will always depend on the *facts* which apply to your housing circumstances, or which apply to a particular housing problem. There are, then, as many descriptions as there are different circumstances and different problems – and that means that there are as many as there are individual readers.

For another thing, many of the rights described in this book have been granted by Act of Parliament. Even though an Act of Parliament may seem to say one thing, judges may interpret it in a way that seems to a lay person completely different. Then again, exactly what an individual contract of tenancy means, or what was agreed or what actually happened, may not be absolutely certain until a judge has considered it, even if it seems clear enough to you.

It is, of course, quite wrong that people's rights should be at all uncertain, whether for these reasons, or because the law changes frequently, or because it seems to you complicated or not to add up to a lot of common sense. It is for these reasons that tenants and other occupiers are often unclear what rights they have, and often frightened to enforce what they think their rights may be, in case it results in them being turned out of their homes.

A related problem is that occupiers often do not know where to turn for advice or help (including legal help), and when they do they sometimes feel that even the advisers can't tell them exactly what their position is.

The principal purpose of this series is to try and help people know what may be available to them, more than it is to tell them exactly what will or may happen in every given situation. The way the series works can best be described by referring to three stages.

The first stage for someone who has a problem, or who just wants to understand his or her situation, is to know that there is, or at the least that there may be, some right, or entitlement, or even a discretion they may be able to take advantage of, and which may benefit them. This series seeks to encourage that knowledge by describing in outline what is available to what class of occupier, in respect of the main problems: security of tenure, paying for housing and disrepair.

The second stage is to claim the benefit of that right, entitlement or discretion. Administrators (or landlords, or others) do not shout aloud about what they are able to do to help, or even always publicize what the law *obliges* them to do to help. It is necessary to ask, and so far as possible to ask with some degree of confidence and accuracy. The series seeks to take the reader far enough to ask, at least in commonplace circumstances: 'isn't it your responsibility to do this, or give me that? Surely, I don't have to leave, or pay that high a rent?' Often, just asking is enough to produce a solution.

Finally, the third stage is when you are still not getting what you want, or you are unsure of what your exact rights are: the landlord is trying to evict you, wants to raise your rent, won't repair, or the local authority will not help you by forcing the landlord to repair, and so on. It is this stage which cannot be covered by this series, because it would require the description of every detail of the whole body of law or administrative provision governing each subject, and covering every possible situation.

It is at this stage that resort must be had to advice agencies or lawyers. The availability – often without cost – of advice is the subject of its own book in this series: the *Lawyer–Client Handbook*. In most areas, there are Citizens' Advice Bureaux, Housing Aid or Action Centres, community groups providing or organizing legal or informed advice, and lawyers who will provide assistance free of charge or at little cost, under the legal aid scheme (see Chapter 10).

Even at this stage, however, this series hopes to help: partly by encouraging the reader to take advice; partly because even lawyers are often not familiar enough with the problems of the people likely to be interested in the class of right or entitlement with which this series is concerned. They may need prodding, to find out or check up on whether 'something can't be done'.

The 'client' (reader) who can open a discussion with an adviser with the proposition that there is 'probably' or even just 'possibly' something which is relevant – using this book to say what – stands a much better chance of securing appropriate advice or aid than the client who cannot.

Against this background, there are a few 'golden rules' which anyone who wants to make sure he or she has the very best chance of getting the most out of the housing rights which are available, without jeopardizing the home, should follow:

1. Always seek advice at the earliest possible opportunity, to check both your exact position and your best tactics.
2. Always keep copies of letters and other documents which you fill in, send or receive. Show them to your adviser.

3. Always keep a note, written as soon as possible afterwards, of any conversations you have with your landlord, his or her agents or employees, or representatives of a local authority. Date it, sign it and keep it. Show it to your adviser.
4. Even if you seem to have the right to do so, do not withhold your rent against something you think you are entitled to, such as works of repair, compensation for damage to your belongings, or a lower rent. Go on paying while you take advice and if necessary obtain a court order which proves what you are entitled to do.
5. Never quit accommodation, for example because of a high rent, disrepair or even just because your landlord tells you to do so, unless you definitely have somewhere else you are certain you want to go to and that you are certain you will be able to live in. Always take advice before quitting.
6. Stand up for your rights. Just because you are your only witness, and/or there is nothing in writing, does not mean that what you say will be disbelieved. Just because it seems difficult to get what you want, don't forget that a little bit of effort trying to establish your rights can sometimes bring substantial housing gains. Don't assume that everyone else – whether a landlord, or the local authority – is right, or more right than you are, or telling you the truth. Always check by taking informed advice.

1: The Language of Housing

What is a tenancy?

A tenancy is the name given to the normal arrangement whereby one person pays money for (i.e. rents) somewhere to live from someone else. The person renting somewhere is the tenant, and the person who rents the premises out is the landlord. Tenancy is a contract, then, rather like any other hiring contract, such as for a car or a television.

Thus, in the same way that someone hiring a car or a television takes over its exclusive use, the tenant takes over the exclusive use of the premises: so long as the tenancy continues, the premises have become the tenant's, and – within reason and the limits described in this book – the tenant can do what he or she likes with them, to the exclusion of all others, including the landlord.

Are all renting arrangements tenancies?

No. Some arrangements under which one person rents accommodation from another are described as 'licences'. Licence means 'permission', and the word is used to distinguish those who rent accommodation from someone else but are not tenants. Those who occupy other people's property without permission are trespassers (sometimes called squatters – see page 34. 'What is a squatter?').

The difference between tenancy and licence is very important in understanding housing rights. Using the same example above, the difference is as major as between renting a car for a period of time, so that it becomes yours to do what you want with, and entering into some other arrangement whereby you have the use of the car, perhaps in common with others, perhaps in common with the owner of the car, perhaps just at specific times or on specific days, or perhaps only so long as you use it within a particular town or area.

Why is the difference between tenancy and licence so important?

Much of this book will be taken up with rights of private tenants which have been created by law: in some cases, this is because the law has always recognized that there is an important distinction between hiring somewhere to live and hiring a car or a television (or, in earlier days, hiring a horse and cart!). So the law implies certain rights into a tenancy arrangement: for example, that the landlord will not unduly interfere with the tenant's right to use, and enjoy, the premises, or that the arrangement can only be brought to an end in one of a specified number of ways. In other cases, Parliament has expressly created rights, such as what rent must be paid, or whether a landlord can evict a tenant at all.

Most of the rights implied by law, or created by Parliament, apply only to *tenants*, not to licensees. Some of the rights apply to both; there are a few rights which belong only to licensees, and do not apply to tenants at all. If you do not know whether you are a tenant or a licensee, you will not know which rights apply to you.

How do I tell the difference between tenancy and licence?

The answer is in two parts. First of all, you have to ask: does the arrangement I have made add up to what the law recognizes as a tenancy? Over the long period of time that English law has been developed, certain rules or principles have evolved, as to what the basic ingredients of tenancy are, and it is therefore necessary to be able to say that the arrangement 'covers' (in other words, includes agreement on) these basic ingredients: this is what I mean when I refer to the arrangement as 'adding up' to what the law will recognize as tenancy.

Secondly, even if all the basic ingredients are present – so that the arrangement *could* qualify as tenancy, it is still necessary to ask: is there something special or peculiar or exceptional about the arrangement which means that although the law *can* recognize the arrangement as tenancy, it will *in fact* describe it as the 'lesser' arrangement of licence?

In *most* cases, the difference is fairly easy to tell. 'Normal' renting arrangements will be tenancies, while there will always be something 'different' about a renting arrangement which is a licence.

In some cases, there will be a written agreement, which describes whether you have a tenancy or a licence. This is not conclusive. Landlords often try to describe tenancies as licences, because licensees have fewer rights than tenants; on the other hand, two people may make an arrangement, which they put in writing and describe as tenancy, and yet the law may say that in truth they have created no more than a licence.

It is essential, then, to learn to tell the difference, even though it is only in a very small minority of cases that a renting arrangement will be licence, and in most cases it will be tenancy.

Does a tenancy or licence have to be in writing?

No. A licence never *has* to be in writing; a tenancy ought to be in writing if it is for a period of three years or more. A normal weekly or monthly tenancy need not be in writing, even if it lasts for more than three years. And even when a tenancy ought to be in writing, it will normally be possible to prove the tenancy with other evidence, such as payment of rent, taking up occupation with the landlord's consent, doing work to the premises.

So writing is not very important, although it is usually helpful to have an agreement in writing, because this may avoid argument on a number of points, including some of those described below.

What are the 'basic ingredients' of tenancy?

The 'basic ingredients' are those points of principle which must be covered by, or agreement as to which must be included in, an arrangement before it can properly be described as a tenancy.

A. Premises

The first ingredient of tenancy is that there must be some premises *of which* to have a tenancy. That is to say, you must be able to describe somewhere and say: 'That is what I have a tenancy of.' You cannot have a tenancy of nowhere, and you cannot have a tenancy that is 'movable'; for instance, the right to sleep in a hostel, but wherever the hostel management puts you cannot amount to a tenancy, because there is nowhere you can say is yours.

The premises can be as little as a room, or as much as a house. You cannot have a tenancy of *half* a room. Commonly, a tenancy will be in a flat – sometimes self-contained, sometimes not self-contained. If the tenancy is in a single room (a bedsitting-room), or sometimes when a flat is not self-contained, you may be sharing such facilities as a bathroom and lavatory with others (including perhaps the landlord if he or she lives in the same house). This is not of itself important, provided there is at least *something* which can be said to 'define' the premises which are the subject of the tenancy.

B. Exclusive possession

The second ingredient of tenancy is that the law will not recognize the arrangement as tenancy unless it is one under which you are given the exclusive use of the premises in question. The law calls this 'exclusive possession'. What is meant in practice is that you have been given the right to use premises as a home, for a period of time, and to the exclusion of all others. This means to the exclusion of others, *including* the landlord. In effect, the premises have been 'turned over to' you for use as a home.

In some cases, such as a house of furnished rooms or flats, a landlord will undertake cleaning services, and to carry these out will reserve a right of entry. If gas or electricity are in the landlord's name, the landlord will again reserve a right to come in. In almost every case, a landlord will reserve the right to come and inspect the condition of the premises, and possibly to carry out repairs, and even where no such right is expressly reserved, the law may imply it.

These rights do not, however, interfere with your 'exclusive possession', because they are limited rights of access, as distinct from a right of *using* the premises. They are for specific purposes, not a general use right. An example of an arrangement under which you have not been given exclusive possession might arise where the landlord has some premises which he or she uses as, for instance, a business store; assuming the arrangement does not give you a specific part of the premises all to yourself, but merely permits you to stay in the house, along with the landlord's stored goods, you will not have the exclusive use or possession of the premises.

The most common examples arise when you are sharing a house or a flat with your landlord, or when a group of you are sharing somewhere. It will be easier to consider these examples as separate questions: 'Will I be a tenant if I am sharing with my landlord? (page 16) and 'Will I be a tenant if I am sharing with someone other than my landlord?' (page 26). Another common example arises when your landlord is also your employer; this, too, is best considered separately – see page 32, 'Will I be a tenant if my landlord is my employer?'

C. *Period of tenancy*

The third essential element in tenancy is that there must be a period of time involved: that is what tenancy is, a slice of time in the use of premises belonging to another. This does not mean that the time must be fixed or definite; a very common form of tenancy is the weekly tenancy, i.e. continuing from week to week, or month to month, until brought properly to an end. There may be a fixed period agreed: three months, six months, a year, and so on.

What it means is that an arrangement under which it is impossible to say that you have been given the right to use the premises for any definable period (or periods) of time at all is not yet a full enough arrangement for the law to recognize as tenancy. Thus, if you need somewhere to sleep for the night, or for a few days, and the landlord agrees to let you stay – perhaps saying that he or she will consider the longer-term position the next day – you will not have a tenancy.

When all else has been agreed, but nothing yet said about time – the arrangement is not sufficiently complete to be called a tenancy. However, as soon as the time factor can be ascertained, the arrangement will have been completed. This may be because there is an express agreement between you and the landlord; or it may be by inference, because you pay rent at some amount per week, or per month. As soon as you do this, your tenancy will have become weekly, or monthly.

D. *Landlord and tenant*

There is a fourth essential ingredient of tenancy: that is, there must be identifiable parties to the arrangement.

This means that there must *be* a landlord, and there must *be* a tenant. You cannot be a tenant of no one; and a landlord cannot let premises to himself or herself. It is a different question from whether you can say who your landlord is (see Chapter 4).

If all of these ingredients are present in the arrangement you have made, you will probably have a tenancy; you will only *not* have a tenancy if there is some other factor present, in addition, which has the effect of *reducing* the arrangement to licence. If any of these four ingredients are missing, however you *cannot* have a tenancy, and therefore – obviously! – you have only a licence. The starting-point, then, is to look at the arrangement, and make sure that all four points are covered, either expressly, or by implication. Do not be daunted by this: if you are living somewhere as a home, they will *usually* be covered, and you will usually be a tenant.

Is rent an essential ingredient of tenancy?

It never used to be considered that whether or not rent was paid was an important element of tenancy. In modern times, however, it has come to be considered that if no rent is payable under the agreement, you are unlikely to be a tenant, because the arrangement will not have the formality, and 'arm's length' quality, which the law assumes will normally be present in tenancy. Put in another way, the *absence* of rent is one of those special or peculiar factors which is *likely* (though not certain) to mean that, even though the other ingredients of tenancy are present, the arrangement is one of licence (see next question).

What are the factors which mean that I may have a licence rather than a tenancy?

If the arrangement does not cover the four basic ingredients of tenancy, you will have a licence. Otherwise, we have to examine the surrounding circumstances, and see whether they mean that the arrangement is in some other way abnormal or exceptional. In answering the last question I have already described one circumstance which would suggest that the arrangement was exceptional: that is, a rent-free arrangement is odd enough to make the law suspect that what you and the landlord had in mind was something less than the full formality of tenancy. (Rent-free arrangements in the context of accommodation related to employment should be considered separately: see page 32, 'Will I be a tenant if my landlord is my employer?')

The second class of circumstance which may be described as exceptional is if you are not a tenant but a lodger. A guest in a hostel might be called a lodger, even though he or she will have his or her own room, perhaps for weeks on end. At the other extreme, you will be a lodger if you are actually living with someone to such an extent that you are treated as part of the family, taking your meals with him or her, and perhaps sharing the living room.

Between these two classes of lodging, there are less obvious cases. If the extent to which the landlord provides you with services – such as cleaning, delivering post, perhaps doing some shopping, or providing your meals – is such that the landlord needs regular, constant access, not merely occasional, or irregular, to the point that the emphasis is shifted from you renting a room or flat to an arrangement under which use of the room or flat is but one of the services you enjoy, then you are likely to be considered a lodger.

Even if you are not a lodger, an arrangement under which the four key elements of tenancy (above) are present may yet not constitute tenancy by reason of exceptional surrounding circumstances if there is some other feature which suggests that it ought not to be so treated. For example, if you are buying a house, but before the purchase is completed you want to enter into occupation, and pay rent for a few weeks, this will not be considered tenancy. An employment-related arrangement (below) may similarly be considered sufficiently 'different' to qualify, exceptionally, as licence, even though the basic ingredients of tenancy are present.

Another example is a charitable arrangement, perhaps where someone has let you into occupation as a favour, at a time of great hardship, even if he or she is charging you a small rent to cover outgoings. This last class of case may be considered in a different way. One might well say that there is no intention to enter into legal relations at all, just as if you are invited to someone's home for dinner and at a late stage your host changes his or her mind and cancels the arrangement you could hardly claim 'breach of contract'.

If your accommodation has been provided by a private landlord, as part of an arrangement with a local authority to whom you have applied for help because you are homeless (see Chapter 2), then again you *may* be considered to be only a licensee.

Hostels (such as YWCA, YMCA) are usually considered to grant licences, rather than tenancies, because the extent to which the 'landlord' retains control – often through quite detailed rules – is quite inconsistent with the idea that what has been created is a separate 'home' within the building, and is closer to 'lodging' (in spirit, even if few services are provided). Of course, sometimes hostels grant only the right to share a room, in which case there could be no tenancy, because there would be no exclusive possession. But often people have their own rooms in a hostel, and for a lengthy period: they would still be licensees. On the other hand, and for example, the YWCA also has a few flats, which *are* separate from their hostels, and a resident in one of these would normally be considered a tenant.

Leaving aside the special cases, such as employer-related accommodation, if the arrangement is at arm's length, and is for *no more nor less than* a straightforward residential arrangement, with not much detail greater than payment of rent in exchange for at least a room of one's own to live in, the arrangement will be considered tenancy.

The most common elements which may preclude a tenancy are: family arrangements, hostels, cohabitation, houses where meals are provided, and acts of kindness or generosity. No example is definitive. It is necessary to get a feel for the circumstances of the arrangement, and if in doubt to take advice.

Will I be a tenant if I am sharing with my landlord?
This question is answered by reference to the same principles we have already considered; are the four ingredients of tenancy present, and is there some other factor which reduces the arrangement to one of licence? The mere fact that your landlord lives in the same house as you is not of itself enough to say that you are only a licensee. On the other hand, it may make a court or other tribunal a bit more likely to look closely at the facts and circumstances of the arrangement, to see if you really do have exclusive possession of any premises as such, i.e. tenancy, or whether in fact you are only a lodger (licensee). If the property is a flat, this will be even more probable than if it is a house.

The examples of circumstances which have to be taken into account will of course be different when you are living in the same house as your landlord from when you are not. The question of whether you are your landlord's tenant or licensee will be answered by examining *how* you live together.

If you have a separate part of your landlord's house,

perhaps even your own kitchen and bathroom, then there is no reason to view the arrangement as anything other than tenancy, even if, for example, you do not have a separate electricity or gas meter, or a separate telephone. This will still be true if all you have rented is a single room, with its own cooking facilities, and are sharing the bathroom and lavatory.

If, however, there is a greater degree of sharing, it will become more likely that you only have a licence. This is why it is more likely that you will be a licensee sharing your landlord's flat, than his or her house – because it is less likely that you live completely separately from him or her. The examples below relate to both houses and flats, but it is common sense that you are more likely to share facilities in flats than houses.

If you share the kitchen, you will probably be a licensee. (A bathroom or lavatory is different from a kitchen: it is visited for a specific purpose, whereas people are more likely to spend time in the kitchen, whether or not actually cooking, and of course more than one person may be using the kitchen at the same time.)

If the arrangement is for you to use the living-room along with your landlord, or a dining-room, it is less and less likely that you will have a tenancy. If you share the costs of basic foods – milk, sugar, bread and so on – again you will probably be thought of as a licensee rather than a tenant. If you share television rental, the same will be true, although sharing the costs of a telephone will probably not have this effect. (The same difference between kitchen and bathroom applies – people may view a television together, while each uses the telephone individually.) If the arrangement is for your landlord to provide you with meals, you will definitely be considered a lodger.

So far, I have discussed matters in terms of a fixed arrangement. Sometimes, however, things change. If a change is minor, a temporary convenience, a single shared item perhaps just on the one occasion, it will make no difference. If, for example, you are ill and your landlord does your shopping, or makes you a meal, it will make no difference: you could as easily do the same for him or her. The law does not attempt to eliminate ordinary neighbourliness.

On the other hand, perhaps because over a period of time you and the landlord become close friends, or decide you are well able to live more closely together, you might agree a whole new arrangement. In such circumstances, the law will decide whether you are a tenant or a licensee by reference to the new arrangement.

Finally, it has to be said that there are few fixed rules. Once the four ingredients of tenancy are established, tenancy is possible; without them, it is not (for instance, if the arrangement is that the landlord will provide you with a room, but can decide which room as and when it pleases him or her). After this you have to look at those facts which indicate whether in truth the landlord was carving out a bit of his or her home and 'transferring' it to you (tenancy), or whether you have been taken in to his or her home to live *with* him or her, as part of his or her household, not just physically within the same four walls (licence.)

Does it make any difference to me if my landlord has a mortgage?

For most purposes, it makes no difference to you that your landlord may have a mortgage on the property in which you live. So long as the mortgage company stays out of the picture, it is completely irrelevant. It will only become relevant if your landlord fails to comply with the terms of the mortgage, in particular if he or she fails to pay the mortgage instalments, and the mortgage company exercise their rights to evict the landlord.

If that should happen, it becomes important to answer two questions. First of all, when was the mortgage taken out? If the mortgage was taken out *after* you went to live in the property, then whatever the mortgage deed says about tenants, your position in relation to the mortgage company will be exactly the same as if they had not evicted the landlord and taken over. They step into the shoes of your landlord.

Secondly, if the mortgage preceded your tenancy, you have to find out whether the mortgage deed forbade the landlord to create tenancies. (It is extremely unlikely to say anything about licences.) If it says nothing, then, again, you are normally in the same position as if the landlord had not been evicted, though if the landlord gave you notice of the mortgage *and* you are what is known as an assured tenant or an assured shorthold tenant (see Chapter 3) you *may* be in the same position as if the mortgage prohibited tenancy. (In *very* rare cases, this could even be so if your assured tenancy preceded the mortgage, or if your landlord did not give you notice: see further Chapter 3.) If the mortgage prohibits the creation of tenancies, however, you will have been an illegal tenant and the mortgage company will be able to evict you by court proceedings without any difficulty. Even though you may have a lot of protection under an Act of Parliament against the landlord (see Chapter 3), it will not help you at all against the mortgage company.

The landlord cannot use the fact that the mortgage deed prohibits tenancies in order to try and get you out, however. He or she cannot rely on the fact that you are an illegal tenant. It is, after all, not your 'wrong' or 'illegality'; it is the landlord who has broken his or her arrangement with the mortgage company. It is for this reason that it will make no difference to you whether or not your landlord has a mortgage *until* the mortgage company takes action against the landlord.

Will I be a tenant if my landlord is only a tenant?

Yes. A landlord is anyone who rents out accommodation to another. This includes another tenant. Indeed, quite a lot of landlords only 'own' property on long leases, and strictly even a long leaseholder is only a tenant in law. It is also not uncommon for people who have rented a whole house, even only on a short periodic or fixed-term tenancy, to let out parts of it to someone else. If your landlord is a tenant, you are called in law a sub-tenant. You will, of course, only be a sub-*tenant* if you are a tenant: you will not be a sub-tenant if you are a *licensee*.

What does it mean if I am a sub-tenant?

If you are a sub-tenant, you are in the same position as any other tenant in most respects. For example, there is no difference deciding whether you are your landlord's tenant or licensee if you share with him or her. In Chapter 3, we shall consider different types of tenancy, and what class of protection you have been given by Parliament; again, it will make no difference to deciding that issue whether your landlord is an owner of the property or merely a tenant. This is the same point that was made in relation to the landlord with a mortgage.

The difference will arise if your landlord quits, whether it is because he or she gives up his or her tenancy, or dies, or is evicted. At this point, the fact that you are a sub-tenant will become very important. In particular, it will become very important to decide whether you are a *legal* sub-tenant or an *illegal* sub-tenant. To decide this it will be necessary to answer two questions: *Was the sub-tenancy illegal to start with? And, even if it was illegal to start with, has it become legal?* It is with this question of whether you are (or have become) a legal sub-tenant or not that I am concerned here: the consequences of the distinction will be described in Chapter 4.

(a) *Legal or illegal to start with?* Many tenancy agreements contain a provision which says that the tenant may not sublet (or 'part with possession' of) the premises. Sometimes the agreement says that there can be no subletting of the whole premises (only), in which case there is no prohibition on subletting part of the premises. More commonly, the agreement says that the tenant cannot sublet the whole *or any part* of the premises.

There are three sorts of prohibition on subletting. First of all there is the sort which simply and baldly states that it is prohibited (either of the whole, or of the whole or part, of the premises). This is called an absolute prohibition. Secondly, there is the sort that says that there can be no subletting without the consent of the landlord. (It may add: 'consent in writing'.) This is called a qualified prohibition.

A qualified prohibition sometimes goes on to say that the landlord cannot withhold consent unreasonably. It does not matter whether or not this is what the agreement says, because (with the exception described below) *all* qualified prohibitions are subject to this provision that the landlord cannot withhold consent unreasonably, as a result of an Act of Parliament (Landlord and Tenant Act 1927).

The third sort of prohibition is a particular type of prohibition which applies only in a limited number of cases. In Chapter 3, we will see that tenancies (and to a lesser extent licences) fall within different classes of security: that is to say, Parliament gives different rights to different people. The principal distinction we will deal with is between protected tenants and assured tenants (who may be ordinary assured tenants, or what is known as assured shorthold tenants). The main difference is that protected tenancies began before 15 January 1989, when the law was changed by the Housing Act 1988, and the others began (with a very small number of exceptions) after that date.

In the case of *periodic* (see above and Chapter 4)

21

assured or assured shorthold tenancies (see Chapter 3), Parliament implies a special kind of prohibition against subletting, *but only in those cases where the tenancy agreement does not itself contain its own provisions*. In other words, if there is nothing in the agreement which either allows you to sublet, or stops you subletting (whether by an absolute or a qualified prohibition – above), then Parliament introduces its own term.

That term *seems* like an ordinary qualified prohibition, because what it says is that you cannot sublet the whole of your premises, or any part of them, without the consent of the landlord. *However*, the normal rule that consent cannot be withheld unreasonably (above) does *not* apply. This means that, however unreasonable it may be to withhold consent, the landlord is entitled to do so. (The exceptions are if the withholding would constitute race or sex discrimination: see Chapter 2.)

I have already described two circumstances when this term is *not* implied: if your tenancy is for a fixed-term (see above and Chapter 4) and if your tenancy agreement covers the question for itself. There is one other circumstance when this term is not implied. You may have been charged a premium – 'key money' – as it is sometimes called, for the grant of this periodic assured tenancy: premiums are prohibited in the case of protected tenancies (see Chapter 2), but they are not prohibited in the case of assured tenancies. For further examples of what constitutes a premium or key money, see page 41.

If you were charged a premium for your tenancy, this special prohibition does not apply: it is presumed that if money has been charged for the tenancy, you and the landlord will have reached your own agreement, and if the landlord does not prevent you subletting, he or she does not intend to do so – for example, it may be thought that by subletting, you may recover some of the cost of the premium. A deposit qualifies as a premium if it is for more than one-sixth of the annual rent (two months' rent).

In Chapters 4 and 5, we will see that where there has been a fixed-term assured tenancy (and – see Chapter 3 – all assured *shorthold* tenancies are fixed-term to begin with), there will normally follow an automatic periodic tenancy 'by extension'. Even if you paid a premium for the original fixed-term, or it contained its own subletting provisions, this special prohibition will apply during the extension periodic tenancy.

With the exception, then, of this special prohibition applicable to periodic assured and assured shorthold tenants, if the agreement says nothing about subletting, you will be entitled to sublet all or part of the premises. The subletting is quite *legal.* If the agreement contains an absolute prohibition on subletting, then on the face of it the subletting will be an illegal subletting.

If the agreement contains an *ordinary* qualified covenant (rather than the special one applicable to assured and assured shorthold tenancies) then whether or not the subletting is legal depends on (a) whether the tenant sought consent for it, and (b) whether consent has unreasonably been withheld by the landlord.

There can be no withholding of consent unless it has been asked for. Therefore, there must *always* be a request (and if the agreement says as much, a request in writing, keeping a copy of the letter), no matter how likely, probable or even certain it is that the landlord will refuse. If the request is in writing, then (Landlord and Tenant Act 1988) the landlord is bound to answer in writing, within a reasonable time, and if he or she refuses consent to give reasons for it.

As a rule of thumb, if the fact that the tenant has a subtenant will make no difference to the landlord, it will be unreasonable to withhold consent. If it would create overcrowding, or overstrain facilities, then even if it makes no day-to-day difference to the landlord, it is likely to be a reasonable refusal.

If the subletting is likely to make a difference to when and whether the landlord is ever allowed to recover the premises (because of statutory protection, see Chapter 3), then it is likely to be reasonable to withhold consent. As usual, it will depend on the facts of each case.

In general, if consent has been refused, it will be for the landlord to show that the refusal was reasonable.

If the prohibition is of the special class only applicable (and only in some circumstances) to assured and assured shorthold tenancies, then if consent is not asked for clearly any subletting will be illegal. If consent is asked for, then whether or not it will be illegal depends on whether or not the landlord consents. There will be nothing you can do about it.

In the case of an ordinary qualified covenant, however, where the landlord's consent is needed, and withheld, there are two courses of action open. Either the tenant can go ahead with the subletting, and you (i.e. the sub-tenant) and the tenant later defend any action the landlord might try to take about it, on the grounds that the subletting was quite proper; or, the tenant can go to court and seek a ruling from the court that the subletting will be reasonable. The latter is by far the safest course of action but as it will take some time, and, because people do not commonly bother with too many formalities, it is rarely done.

Note, however, that whether or not a subletting to you is legal or illegal does not affect the arrangement as between you and the tenant (your landlord). The *tenant* has committed the 'wrong', not you, because it was his or her agreement that was broken. The tenant cannot then take advantage of his or her own wrong, and try to use it (for instance, as a reason for eviction) against you. Unless and until the landlord takes action about it, your position will be the same either way.

(b) Has it become legal? Even if a subletting is illegal, it may *become* legal after it has begun. This will happen if, *knowing that there has been a breach of the tenancy agreement,* the landlord condones the breach, by doing nothing about it, and, usually, just going on taking the rent in the normal way. Just as the tenant cannot take advantage of his or her own wrong and try to use the illegality of the subletting against you, the landlord cannot 'save up' the wrong until it suits to use it.

When there has been a breach of a tenancy agreement, as in this case by illegal subletting, and the landlord condones it, it is said that the breach has been 'waived', i.e. it is no longer treated as a breach. The breach which has been waived may be of an absolute prohibition on subletting, or of a qualified prohibition.

The essential elements of 'waiver' of breach are that the landlord (a) knows of the breach, and (b) in a positive sense does nothing about it. The landlord may know directly, or indirectly through an 'agent', whether formally the letting or managing agent, or through, for example, a caretaker of a block of flats.

It may even be that the landlord does not *in fact* know, but that the landlord is treated as knowing, because the subletting was known to someone who *ought* to have told him or her. Thus, the fact that someone who comes to the premises on behalf of the landlord to carry out repairs knows about the subletting will not help; on the other hand, it is part of a caretaker's job to keep an eye on a block of flats, and if subletting is going on, the caretaker ought to have told the landlord. Even if the caretaker has failed to do so, the tenant (and you) can claim that the landlord 'knew' (because, after all, the failure was on the landlord's 'side').

As for 'doing nothing about it', this must be, at least to some extent, a 'positive' failure. Doing nothing for a few weeks or, possibly, months, will not add up to condoning the breach. The landlord may still be in the process of arranging action, or writing a letter telling the tenant to get rid of you; and similarly doing nothing for a while is still likely to leave the landlord with the right to follow up the breach. But if, knowing or deemed to have known of the breach, the landlord does nothing for a lengthy period of time, a decision to condone the breach will be implied.

The most common form of waiver is acceptance of rent, in the knowledge of the breach. None the less, waiver need not be by way of acceptance of rent: it can be by any act of the landlord (or an omission of such significance or period as to be deemed to be a positive act) which demonstrates, or is treated as demonstrating, that the breach has been waived. Once the breach has been waived, your sub-tenancy will be treated as if it was a legal sub-tenancy.

Will I be a tenant if I am sharing with someone other than my landlord?

Slightly different problems arise in deciding whether or not you have a tenancy when you are sharing with someone other than your landlord. It will be easiest to describe these problems if we assume that you are sharing (whether a flat or a house, or, indeed, even a single room) with just one other person, rather than with several others. The position will be no different however many of you there are.

The choice here is between (a) being one of two joint tenants (in other words, you and the person with whom you are sharing), or (b) each of you being a licensee of the landlord, or (c) one of you being a tenant, with the other being his or her licensee, or (d) each of you being a tenant of a special part of the premises (e.g. a room), of the landlord. There is nothing strange or unusual about joint tenancy. What it means is that 'the' tenant is in fact two persons: *between* you both, you have exclusive possession, and all the other essential ingredients of tenancy, *unless* there is some other factor which reduces the arrangement to licence (such as family arrangement and so on).

If you and your would-be joint tenant approach the landlord together, to find somewhere to live together, and the landlord agrees to rent the two of you some premises, there will be no difference between the position of the two of you and any sole tenant. The same questions are asked, and the answers determine whether or not you have a tenancy at all. It will be a point of almost incidental information that you are joint tenants.

Between you, you enjoy all the rights of tenancy, as against the landlord. You do not enjoy the right to, for example, half of the premises each, nor are you (at least usually) only liable for half the rent (although in an odd case a landlord and joint tenants may agree that this is how the rent will be paid, and that fact alone may not prevent the arrangement being one of joint tenancy). Neither one of you can evict the other: if one of you wants to leave, and the other does not, problems *can* arise (see Chapter 4) but there is no need for this to be the case and normally it will be possible for just one of you to remain.

If at the outset, you are the one who has had all the dealings with the landlord, he or she may wish to suggest that *you* alone are the tenant, and your co-occupier merely your licensee. He or she will particularly wish to do this if you leave, for this will mean that he will be able to evict the other (because it is *tenants* not licensees who have the major rights to remain: see Chapter 3). If there is a written agreement and this names the two of you, you will be the joint tenants, and it will be difficult to the point of impossibility for the landlord to say that only one of you is the tenant, and the other your licensee.

If, on the other hand, a written agreement or, for example, a rent book names only one of you, it is also difficult (although not *quite* to the same extent) to show that in fact the arrangement was for a joint tenancy. You could only do this by showing (a) that the landlord knew who you intended to share with, *and* (b) intended that your co-occupier should be a joint tenant with you, *and* (c) his or her name has been left off either by mistake or with the deliberate intention of creating a false impression.

If there is *no* written agreement, or rent book with only one name on it, it is less hard to show that you are both joint tenants. It becomes a question of fact: who was the landlord dealing with? One or both of you? The mere fact that only one of you may actually have *met* the landlord is not conclusive; it may have been a question of convenience or may have been accidental, the landlord may have taken down full details, or even sought references from both of you.

If the landlord seeks references from both of you, that is good, strong and clear evidence of intention to create a joint tenancy (rather than that only one of you should be the tenant, and the other his or her licensee), unless, of course, the results were extremely adverse for one of you and the landlord in consequence would only agree to the other becoming the tenant. If the landlord addresses rent *demands* to both of you, that is good evidence of joint tenancy, although the mere fact that both of you *pay* the rent, for instance on alternate rent days, or out of a joint account, does not amount to quite such good evidence, because the landlord is entitled to his or her rent and can claim he or she was only accepting it from the non-tenant on behalf of the tenant.

Other evidence, like names on gas, telephone or electricity bills, is less useful, because the landlord is unlikely to have known about those arrangements. Evidence arising out of disrepair (requests for repairs, arrangements for access and so on) can help but is probably classed like rent payments as something the landlord can claim he or she understood to have been on behalf of the named tenant or tenants. If the only evidence available is the written agreement or rent book, or if the only evidence is of an oral agreement reached in person, it must be said that it is hard to convince a court that the landlord is so careless about his or her business that he or she has made a formal arrangement of tenancy with someone he or she knows nothing about.

One common problem which arises is when one of the joint tenants leaves, and the remaining one wants to replace him or her with someone else, as *joint tenant*. This will need the landlord's permission. After all, you cannot really expect to be able to *impose* a tenant on a landlord against his or her will. If the landlord is not willing to accept a replacement occupier as tenant, it will normally be possible for you to bring him or her in as a licensee (see Chapter 6). If the landlord *is* willing to accept a replacement joint tenant, then there will be a new tenancy, although there is no reason why this should not be, in all other respects, merely a continuation of the former tenancy.

Most commonly, however, no one approaches the landlord. One person goes, another comes in; gradually, the turnover can result in none of the original tenants being left in occupation. Have the new occupiers become tenants? The answer is that probably they have not. There has to be strong evidence – of the same sort as described above in relation to establishing who the original joint tenants are – that the landlord has accepted the new occupier as one of the tenants; for example, a long period of payment of rent by the incoming occupier, or extensive dealings, or other circumstances which show that the landlord knew that this person had taken over from someone else, rather than was merely living with an existing tenant.

The landlord *may* try, however, to set up an arrangement which is not joint tenancy *at all*, so that none of these questions arise. There may be an attempt to get you and your co-occupier to sign a particular form of agreement which has come to be called a 'non-exclusive occupation agreement'. Under this sort of agreement, the landlord gives – or purports to give – each of you a separate right: to live in the premises but not in any particular part of them; to share the premises with whomsoever the landlord nominates (which will 'happen' to be the other one of you); to pay a separate 'rent' for occupation; and so on.

What the landlord is trying to do is to destroy any tenancy. Individually, neither of you has a tenancy, either of the whole of the premises (in which others, too, are to live) or even of any particular room (because the agreement says not). Together, you do not have the possession of the whole premises, because it is not you who, under the agreement, are to decide who can use them, but the landlord. The non-exclusive occupation agreement, then, seeks to set up a licence instead of (joint) tenancy.

This used to be a most common device, but recently the courts have expressed their disapproval of such agreements, and suggested that if a number of people approach the landlord to share premises, paying rent for them, so that on the face of it all the normal ingredients of tenancy (above) are present, there will be a joint tenancy, whatever the individual agreements say. A non-exclusive occupation agreement will *only* work if the different sharers are chosen by the landlord, who also chooses replacement sharers; even then, if the landlord allocates specific rooms to the individual sharers, each may well have a sole tenancy of that room.

The reason the courts will not uphold a non-exclusive occupation agreement made between the landlord and the individual members of a couple or a group is that the law considers it to be a 'pretence' or 'sham' or 'false label' designed to get around the statutory protection described in Chapter 3 and most of which applies only to tenants.

What 'pretence' or 'sham' means is that while the written agreement says one thing, what the parties (you, your co-occupier and the landlord) *intended* was something different. It may sound, at this stage, surprising to think in terms of people intending one thing, but drawing up a written agreement that says something else. Actually, it is common. The reason landlords want to do it is because licensees have much, much less security than tenants (including joint tenants). The reason tenants agree to sign the forms is because they are desperate for somewhere to live.

Normally what happens is that a couple of you approach the landlord and find that he or she has somewhere appropriate for you to live. Rent is agreed, and a date when the occupation can commence. Then the landlord asks you each to sign one of these documents. (It will always involve separate documents, because the landlord is trying to show that you are separate, not 'joint'). If you raise any queries, he or she (or it may be an agent acting for the landlord) says: 'Don't worry; it's just a form. You'll really be left alone to live together.'

Nevertheless, there the written agreements are, and on their face they give you few rights and the landlord many – including, specifically, the right to put other people in to live with you, in addition or in replacement, and even to come and live in the premises himself or herself should he or she please. If the agreements are approached coldly, having no regard to the true position, one would be forced to say: 'well, this cannot be tenancy because none of you alone, nor all of you together, have got exclusive possession.' You will reply: 'But that wasn't what was meant!' The question is: which prevails – that which was in writing, or what was really meant? The answer is that if it is a pretence or devise to get around statutory protection, what was meant is what will prevail.

The court will look at everything that has gone on

before and up to and including the time the agreement was signed, and even how you have lived, and how the agreement has operated since. *Only* if the court finds that it was really intended that the landlord should choose the sharers will you fail to establish joint tenancy.

Is there such a thing as joint sub-tenancy?

Yes. None of the matters I have described excludes any of the others. You can have a joint tenancy, which is a sub-tenancy, living in the same house as your landlord, and the landlord can have a mortgage on the property! It may be a legal or an illegal tenancy in relation to the mortgage, and a legal or illegal sub-tenancy! There may be a non-exclusive occupation agreement in the landlord's house, or a couple may live together as such, and be licensees in the landlord's house for some other reason altogether, i.e. because they together also live in a close arrangement with the landlord. Just consider for a moment the position of a child who brings into the family home his or her spouse or cohabitant: they would not become joint tenants of the parents just for that reason, any more than the child would have been his or her parents' tenant or sub-tenant to begin with.

Will I be a tenant if my landlord is my employer?

When you live in property owned by your employer, you are sometimes described as occupying tied accommodation. Tied accommodation is, in some respects, a law unto itself although, once facts and circumstances are examined from this different approach, it will be seen that the basic *principles* are exactly the same as those applicable in the ordinary case of needing to distinguish whether someone is a tenant or a licensee, i.e. are all the four ingredients of tenancy present, and, if so, is there some other feature which shows that no tenancy was intended? (This subject is considered in greater detail in *The Tied Occupiers Handbook* in this series.)

The term 'tied accommodation' is not a legal term. It is generally used to mean accommodation which 'goes with the job'. Quite a lot of people get accommodation from their employers: not only the obvious classes such as caretakers, porters, nurses, hotel workers, resident wardens in hostels and old people's schemes, resident housekeepers, other living-in help, but also pub managers, some managers of off-licences, the employees of some of the larger industries, such as railways, the Coal Board, London Transport; even some teachers and social workers are offered accommodation by their employers.

There are three classes of case which have to be distinguished. First, you may need to live in particular accommodation in order to carry out your work (or, even if you do not need to live in particular accommodation, it is manifestly more convenient for you to do so, *and* as a term of your employment, your employer requires you to live there, in order to carry out your duties better). In this case, your 'job requirements' take precedence over any of the considerations otherwise discussed, and you are a licensee because the overriding intention is job-related. This class of occupation is known as 'service occupation'. Most of those described in the last paragraph, other than employees of large industries, teachers and social workers, are likely to fall into this class.

Secondly, you may be offered accommodation when you are taking up employment, because your new employer has accommodation available and you need somewhere to live. In this class of case, it is incidental that your landlord is your employer, and although you are known as a service tenant, you have a proper tenancy. (There may, however, be an issue over (a) what sort of statutory protection applies to you, if you are provided with the accommodation rent-free in exchange for lower wages – see Chapter 3, and (b) the extent of your security – see Chapter 5.) The fact that your accommodation is rent free, or that your rent is deducted from your wages, will not in this case have the effect described earlier of making a tenancy into a licence (because there is an 'explanation' for no rent which is still consistent with a 'formal' or 'arm's length' intention). The others described above will normally fall into this class.

Finally, you may fall into housing need and happen to secure accommodation from an existing employer, or you may fall into employment need and secure a job from your landlord. In neither case should this be considered as 'tied' accommodation at all. It is largely a coincidence that your employer happens to have accommodation available, or that your landlord has a job free.

If it is the first way around, then only a finding that the right of occupation was granted as a particular favour (for instance, when your employer would otherwise not have let out the accommodation at all, or might have sold it or rented it out at a high rent under a different kind of agreement) should turn the tenancy into licence, on the same principles considered above: that the arrangement was exceptional. If it is the second way around, then the fact that you go to work for your landlord should make no difference at all to the nature of your occupation (unless it can be said that you have given up an existing tenancy, in favour of a wholly new arrangement, under which either you have become a service occupier, or in some other way 'tenancy' has been overridden).

What is a squatter?

The term 'squatter' is not a legal term. It is popularly used to refer to people who *either* occupy someone else's property without permission, *or* people who occupy property, which is shortly to be redeveloped, on a temporary basis, but with permission. Occupying someone else's property without permission is *trespass*. Occupying property which is shortly to be redeveloped, with permission, but probably paying no or only nominal rent, is either tenancy or licence, and it will usually be considered licence because of the circumstances of the occupation, i.e. because no rent or only nominal rent is charged, and because the only reason you have been allowed in is on account of impending redevelopment.

You will be a trespasser, therefore, if you have no permission to be on property from someone who has the power to grant that permission. For example, if an existing tenant allows you to come into the property, as a licensee, you will not be a trespasser, even if the landlord does not want you to be there, because the exclusive possession of the property has become the tenant's, and he or she has the right to give permission to use it.

Conversely, if a landlord gives you permission to occupy property which in fact is already subject to someone else's tenancy, *you* will be a trespasser. (Putting someone else into tenanted property is a not uncommon form of harassment.) Indeed, a landlord can be a trespasser in his own or her own tenant's property, if he or she does not have a tenant's permission, or some other legal right, to be on the premises.

You will *not* be a trespasser if you do have permission from someone with authority to let you in: for example, an owner or an owner's agent. It can be difficult to tell if someone who gives you permission to enter does in fact have authority to do so. As a general proposition, if it can be shown that the owner has some responsibility for making you believe that the agent had authority to let you in, even though in fact the agent did not have such authority, the owner will be fixed with his or her agent's actions (that means that you will be treated as having permission, and will not be a trespasser).

2: Getting Somewhere to Live

How do I find somewhere to live?
Finding somewhere to live, if you do not have the money for purchase (with or without a mortgage) is extremely difficult.

If you are homeless, and you or someone you live with has children, or is pregnant, or elderly or vulnerable because of physical or mental handicap, the local authority for the area in which you live may have a duty to find you somewhere to live, under the Housing Act 1985. You should certainly apply to it. If it is able to say that you have become homeless through your own fault, however, it may be able to avoid this duty. It is for this reason, as well as the grave shortage of available rented accommodation, that you should try never to quit anywhere without somewhere else to move to.

In fact, anyone can apply to the local authority, but with the exception of a few progressive areas where some provision is made for the young, single or childless, it is likely to be a long time before anywhere is found for those who do not qualify under the Housing Act. There may be a better chance of applying to a housing association or trust. Both authorities, and associations/trusts, sometimes make available property which is scheduled for redevelopment, on short-life licences (see Chapter 1).

Access to the public sector is, however, highly prized, because the quality of rented accommodation in the public sector is likely to be better than in the private sector, and because, regardless of *legal* protection, you are likely to be better treated as a public tenant than as a private tenant. (As a general proposition, there can be equal or even greater inefficiency in the public sector, but there is not commonly the ill-will, nor harassment, that mars the private sector.)

In this book, we are concerned with access to private-sector accommodation. In brief, accommodation is found howsoever you can. Aside from word-of-mouth, you may be able to find accommodation through newspaper or magazine advertisements, cards in shop windows, or accommodation or estate agents.

Is a tenancy or licence valid if granted by an agent?

Yes. It is not necessary for you to meet or deal with a prospective landlord directly. Indeed, it is quite common to have nothing to do with a landlord other than through agents, both when taking premises or later when paying rent and if trying to get repairs done.

A landlord will be bound by the acts of his agents, including in the grant of a tenancy or licence. For these purposes, 'agent' refers to anyone who is acting on behalf of the landlord, not just someone who formally calls himself or herself an 'estate agent' or 'accommodation agent'.

If a dispute arises as to whether or not someone really is or was the landlord's agent, and it is shown that formally that person was *not* acting with the landlord's authority, you may still be able to fix the landlord with the consequences of the agent's actions, including the grant of a right of occupation, if the landlord had some responsibility for letting you believe the agent was properly authorized, i.e. if the landlord has – or is deemed to have – 'held out' the agent as acting for him or her.

Do I have to pay an agent for finding me somewhere to live?

Yes, but only if and when the agent is successful in finding you somewhere to live (Accommodation Agencies Act

1953). It is a criminal offence for anyone to *demand or accept* any payment for *registering the requirements* of a prospective *tenant*. This applies when the agency says they will make a charge for the service of recording your requirements, i.e. 'taking you on to their books'. Note, however, that if the agency even so much as asks for such a payment, as much as if payment is accepted, the offence has been committed.

It is also a criminal offence to *demand or accept* any payment for supplying *addresses or other details* of property to let. This means the agency can make no charge merely for supplying addresses or other details. The agency *can* charge, however, for actually arranging a letting. In effect, then, no money should be asked for or taken until somewhere is found.

One difficulty with these – and other 'protective' – provisions is that if you make a fuss, it is likely to result in a refusal to find you somewhere to live. The provisions are best kept for when a payment has been sought and made, and you cannot get it back when nowhere is found for you. You would also be within your rights to report an agency which either charged you additional, illegal sums or asked for money too early, once somewhere has been found and you are safely in occupation.

If you have cause to complain, the proper authority to take the matter to is the Tenancy Relations or Harassment Officer of the local authority. They may prosecute an offence and in the course of the prosecution demand the return of your money; you may also take civil proceedings, in a county court, on your own behalf, for the return of any money which was illegally demanded from you.

Can a landlord or agent refuse to rent me somewhere?

Yes, *other* than if the refusal is on account of racial or

sexual discrimination. Because we are dealing with private landlords, they are basically free to do what they want, except so far as the law intervenes. The law tells some public landlords (i.e. local authorities) whom they have to help (see page 37, 'How do I find somewhere to live?'), but not private landlords.

However, private landlords – like everyone else – are covered by the Race Relations Act 1976 and the Sex Discrimination Act 1975. This means that they cannot discriminate against you on the grounds of colour, race, nationality, ethnic or national origins, or sex (i.e. female or male), either directly or indirectly, by introducing a condition into a letting which is not justifiable on some grounds other than race or sex, and which makes it more difficult for you, because of your race or sex, to take up the accommodation.

Thus, it would be illegal to refuse you accommodation, or to give you a lower priority, or to require that someone else guarantees your rent, in a way that would not be sought were it not for your race or sex. It would be illegal to allocate rooms in one house to people of one race or sex and those in another house to people of another (save that, in the case of sex, the latter class of discrimination is legal if the accommodation includes shared dormitories or sleeping accommodation, or shared washing or sanitary facilities. There is also a general exception for 'single-sex charities').

It is also illegal for a landlord to refuse consent to a subletting (see Chapter 1) or assignment (see page 42, 'Can I take over someone else's tenancy or licence?') on racial or sexual grounds, to advertise in a discriminatory way, to instruct an employee or agent to discriminate illegally, or to put pressure on someone to discriminate (for instance, a landlord telling an agent that he or she will get no more work from him or her unless he or she discriminates).

There is an exception to the provisions which relates to what are called 'small premises', where the landlord or a near relative (spouse, parent, child, grandparent, grandchild, brother or sister) lives in the same building, and shares some extent of accommodation (including a bathroom, lavatory, kitchen or living-room, but not including mere means of access or storage space) with other occupiers. 'Small premises' are those where *either* there is no room for more than six occupiers (other than the landlord or relative and members of his or her family), i.e. in individual rooms, *or*, in a house let off in flats, where there are no more than two flats (other than occupied by landlord or relative).

As with so many other housing 'rights', laws preventing this or that action sound all very well, and operate in your interests, so long – and only so long – as landlords and their agents and employees obey them. The provision the law makes for 'backing up' its provisions are usually inadequate: even if a landlord is fined for an illegal act, or if you can go to court for an order against the landlord, long periods of time may pass, during which you may have no housing. The very mention of 'rights', rather than resulting in obedience to law (whether or not for fear of consequences), may instead cause the loss of your chance to get somewhere to live.

Whether or not to use rights, then, is a matter for you. The risk of loss of benefit must be weighed up; so also must the extent to which you can end up without a particular benefit but bogged down in legal or similar procedures. On the other hand, if *no one* uses what is available, things do not change for others; and sometimes, positive gains may be obtained in individual cases by standing up for your rights.

In the case of discrimination, there are two bodies – the Commission for Racial Equality, and the Equal Opportunities Commission – which exist in order to try and enforce these laws. Anyone can take a complaint direct to the appropriate organization, and each organization maintains staff to investigate and pursue cases, either by informal means or by pressing claims through the courts. Alternatively, you are entitled to take action by civil proceedings in the county court, on your own behalf.

The law on these subjects is considered in greater detail in *The Race Discrimination* and *The Sex Discrimination Handbooks* in this series.

Can I take over someone else's tenancy or licence?

You cannot take over someone else's licence, because a licence is a personal permission. Some tenancies cannot be assigned, and some can. So much depends on the type of tenancy that this question is best dealt with in Chapter 6 (under the question 'Can I transfer my tenancy or licence to someone else permanently?', page 137), after we have defined the different types of tenancy and security.

Can I inherit a tenancy or licence?

You cannot inherit a licence, because a licence is a personal permission. Special provisions are made for the inheritance of protected and assured tenancies. There are general provisions under which you may be able to inherit another tenancy but, as with the last question, it will be easier to consider this in Chapter 6, under the question 'Can my family take over my tenancy or licence?' (page 140) after defining different types of tenancy and security.

Do I have to pay key money or a deposit?

Key money is the name given to a payment, other than rent or other outgoings, which is just for the privilege of being granted a tenancy or licence. Another name for key money is 'premium'. A *deposit* is a sum of money sought by a landlord, at the commencement of a tenancy or licence, by way of 'security' against any one of a range of incidents, such as non-payment of rent, damage to property, or removal of furniture.

There is no general prohibition on charging someone either key money or a deposit when granting them a tenancy or a licence, whether the tenancy or licence is granted by a landlord, or in those circumstances in which it is permissible to take over someone else's tenancy. However, there are provisions which apply to the following classes of occupation: protected tenancies, protected shorthold tenancies and, in some cases, restricted contracts (Rent Act 1977). To find out if what you have been given is within one of these classes, see Chapter 3. The provisions only apply to restricted contracts if a rent has been registered by a Rent Tribunal (and not removed from the register): see Chapter 8. Because (subject only to minor exceptions) there can be no *new* tenancies/contracts of these classes after 15 January 1989 (see Chapter 3), we are therefore only concerned with a premium you may have paid in the past, or on the assignment of an existing tenancy.

The provisions permit a limited deposit, and key money only in tightly defined circumstances, and also only to a limited extent.

A deposit is permitted (a) if it is of a reasonable amount in relation to the purpose for which it is claimed (for example, an amount which is said to be for protection against damage to furniture must be reasonable in relation to the amount of furniture involved), *and* (b) if it is of no more than one-sixth of the annual rent (i.e. two months' rent, which is, however, slightly more than eight weeks' rent if the rent is charged weekly).

Both these criteria must be fulfilled, so that a deposit of two months' rent in respect of a small amount of furniture, worth much less than two months' rent, would not be permitted. The deposit ought to be returned at the end of the tenancy, subject to any proper deduction, and, if it is not, can be sued for like any other debt one person may owe another.

A deposit which does not fall within these limits is likely to be considered 'key money', even if it is said that you will get it back at the end of the tenancy. Key money is normally a cash sum, but anything that could be quantified in cash terms can be considered key money, such as making you buy some goods for the person demanding the money, or making you forego a debt which is owed you by the person demanding the money. In one case, a firm of estate agents said that they would buy a house from some people, at one price, but offered to find a tenancy for them elsewhere, paying a reduced purchase price for the house. The reduction was held to be a form of key money.

One common form of 'premium' is when a price is asked for 'fixtures and fittings'. This is now more commonly asked by an outgoing tenant than by a landlord. It is not key money if no more is asked for than the fixtures and fittings, or furniture, are worth; any excessive price asked for or received is, however, illegal key money. Anyone seeking to make you pay for furniture has to provide a priced inventory of it, and it is illegal to fail to do so.

An outgoing tenant can also ask for a proportion of costs of installing fixtures, or making alterations, and of any outgoings, such as rates, telephone rental or standing charges for gas and electricity, which are applicable to the period after the change.

It is already clear that it is not only landlords who demand key money but also outgoing tenants. An estate agent may do so on behalf of either a landlord or an outgoing tenant. In one case, an outgoing tenant charged not for the transfer of the tenancy, but for arranging for the landlord to grant a new tenancy. It was still held to be within the provisions prohibiting key money.

The act of asking for, or receiving, an illegal premium is a criminal offence, and the money paid is recoverable by civil action at any time within six years of payment, just as one might try to recover any other debt. Offences may be reported to, and prosecuted by, the Tenancy Relations or Harassment Officer of the local authority.

If you are asked for key money by an outgoing tenant under a protected tenancy or restricted contract, you will probably not want to refuse, or to raise objections, for fear of losing the letting. There is nothing improper in paying the money, knowing that you will be able, and intending, to claim it back later. This problem cannot arise with a protected shorthold tenancy, as such a tenancy cannot be transferred by an outgoing tenant (see Chapter 6).

How much rent will I have to pay in advance?

The short answer is that you may be asked for any amount in advance, *unless* what you have been given is a protected or protected shorthold tenancy (see Chapter 3). Again, we are here only concerned with tenancies already granted (see Chapter 3). It is illegal to charge a protected or protected shorthold tenant any rent at all before the first day of the period for which the rent is being paid, in other words before the first day of the week for a weekly tenancy, or of the month for a monthly tenancy (Rent Act 1977).

It is a criminal offence to attempt to charge rent in breach of these provisions, which mean that for the normal, weekly protected tenancy only one week at a time need be paid. If you do pay rent in advance where you do not need to do so, you can reclaim it from the landlord, or set it off against future rent. It would seem, however, that once the beginning of the period has come around again, the rent will become due, so that there is little advantage to you in these provisions, unless very large advance payments have been required.

If a landlord enters up a rent book *as if* you were in arrears with the rent, because of an improper requirement to pay rent in advance, it is a criminal offence and, at your request, the landlord is obliged to delete the wrongful entry within seven days, or he or she will be committing yet another offence. All of these offences may be reported to, and may be prosecuted by, the Tenancy Relations or Harassment Officer of the local authority.

Am I entitled to a rent book?

If under the arrangement you are to pay your rent weekly, you will be entitled to be provided by the landlord with a rent book, or some other similar document (Landlord and Tenant Act 1962). The one exception to this is if the rent includes payment for board, and the value of the board forms a substantial part of the whole rent paid: this is a formula used in defining certain tenants who are excluded from being protected tenants or having restricted contracts, because of the provision of board (see Chapter 3).

Rent books, or other similar documents, have to contain certain information: name and address of landlord; and information prescribed by the government. The information prescribed includes particulars as to agents acting on behalf of the landlord, rent, rent registrations, terms of contracts and rights such as those to share facilities. In addition, the rent book must contain details on the overcrowding laws (see Chapter 6). Where the landlord is a limited company, you are entitled to require the company to provide the names and addresses of all directors and of the secretary to the company.

It is a criminal offence for a landlord to fail to comply with these requirements, but the failure to provide you with a rent book does not permit the occupier to withhold the rent. The offence may be reported to the local authority Tenancy Relations or Harassment Officer, although of course you will not wish to do this until you have taken up occupation, and you may not wish to do so even then if you have little security of tenure, for instance, if you a licensee (see Chapter 5).

How do I find out who my landlord is?

When you take a tenancy, you may do so from an agent. It may not be clear who your landlord is – if there is no written agreement, for example, or if you do not have a rent book. Even if there is a written agreement or rent book, the details may only give you the name of the agent to whom you are to pay the rent, or some other manager.

As a tenant, but not as a licensee, you are entitled to make a written request to the last person who demanded rent from you, or to the last person to whom you paid the rent, or to anyone else who is acting as your landlord's agent in relation to your tenancy, to be told your landlord's name and address (Landlord and Tenant Act 1985). It is a criminal offence for that person to fail to provide you with this information, in writing, within twenty-one days of your request. If the answer is that the landlord is a company, you can make a further request, but this time to the landlord company, for information about who its directors and secretary are, and again it is a criminal offence to fail to answer within twenty-one days.

These offences may be reported to the local authority's Tenancy Relations or Harassment Officer, who may prosecute them, and who may also be able to use other powers to find out who is responsible for premises. A licensee who has lost track of his or her landlord may be able to get help from the local authority, using these other powers, to find out who the landlord is. These powers, then, can be used once you have taken up occupation.

What happens if my landlord changes after I take up occupation?

If you are a tenant, and once you have taken up occupation, it will normally make no difference to you if your landlord sells his or her interest to someone else. It can have the effect of moving you from one class of statutory protection to another, but this may well be a change for the better (see Chapter 3). The new landlord is obliged to inform you in writing within two months of the sale that it has taken place and what his or her name and address is (Landlord and Tenant Act 1985). It is a criminal offence to fail to comply with this obligation, and it may be reported to the local authority's Tenancy Relations or Harassment Officer.

If you are a licensee, however, unless the new landlord is prepared to let you go on living in the premises, your right of occupation will normally be considered to have come to an end. In practice, licences will usually occur in circumstances which will mean you will be told before any such sale, and probably asked to leave.

How do I find out the terms of my occupation?

Most of the important terms of your occupation are the subject of later chapters of this book: security of tenure is described in Chapters 4 and 5, who is entitled to live in the premises in Chapter 6, rents in Chapters 7 and 8, and repairs and improvements in Chapters 9 and 10. The provisions described in those chapters will usually override what you have actually agreed, so far as they are in conflict.

Otherwise, if there is an agreement in writing, this will contain the terms of the letting and, provided it does not contain anything offensive to public policy (such as requiring of you illegal or immoral acts), you are obliged to comply with the agreement. If you break a term of the agreement, the landlord may be able to bring your tenancy to an end and evict you, although if the breach is a minor breach, this is unlikely to happen, at least without you being given an opportunity to make amends. Indeed, if the term is trivial, the courts may entirely ignore any breach. (See, generally, Chapters 4 and 5.)

If there is no written agreement but there is a rent book, this may well contain terms of tenancy. It is the terms that appear in the *first* rent book which matter, rather than any later rent book that may be used, although if earlier rent books cannot be found with which to demonstrate that some term or other now appearing was not in the first book, it may be that you will be stuck with the later entry. Changes of this sort tend not to happen deliberately, but because the landlord buys rent books from a stationer, and over a period of time the standard clauses which are printed in the back of the rent books may have altered.

If there is neither written agreement, nor rent book, then there are only two sources of information as to what the terms of the letting are. First of all, either you or the landlord may claim that something or other was agreed orally. This will be acceptable evidence, and it is wrong to assume that just because it is not in writing, or just because it is your word against his or hers, you will not be believed. Secondly, the law itself implies certain terms into tenancies, and licences, which will apply in any event: for example, in a tenancy, that the landlord will not interfere with your right to use the premises in a proper and decent manner; and, in a licence, that you will be able to use the premises for the purposes the licence was granted. Repairs terms are described in Chapter 9.

What will I have to pay for gas and electricity?
If you have a direct arrangement with the Gas or Electricity Boards, i.e. the accounts are in your name, you will pay the same as anyone else. However, especially in

bedsitting-rooms, and not uncommonly in a house subdivided into flats, the meters will be in the landlord's name, whether or not they are coin meters.

Regardless of whether you are a tenant or a licensee, you will only have to pay the maximum which these Boards say. The Electricity Board is entitled to publish a 'tariff', which can differ from area to area, setting out the maximum amounts at which the electricity may be charged for on resale, i.e. by a landlord to a tenant. Most areas have in fact used this power. The Gas Board is obliged to fix maximum prices governing resale. Both Boards publish the tariffs, so that, if you want to know what you *ought* to be paying, you can obtain the tariff from the Board and work out whether or not you are being overcharged.

If the landlord is overcharging you for gas or electricity, you can sue for the money which you can show to have been in excess of the allowed limits, and can also obtain a court order to compel the landlord to continue the services at the proper price. Of course, the exercise of this right is in practice much more available if you have adequate security of tenure than if you do not, for you may otherwise find that by using your rights you have provoked a notice to quit (see Chapter 4).

3: Class of Security

What does 'class of security' mean?
In Chapter 1, I described the difference between tenancy and licence (and, incidentally, trespass). The differences have existed for many centuries. In this century, however, Parliament has passed a number of Acts which have given some tenants and some licensees a number of important rights. These rights include the possibility not merely of continuing to live somewhere for the whole of your life but even to pass a tenancy on to your children, and in some cases then to your grandchildren. The rights also include some controls on what rents may be charged you. (In practice, there would be no point in letting you live somewhere as long as you wanted if the landlord could charge what rent he or she liked; nor much value in limiting rents if the landlord could evict you at will.)

Not all private tenants have the same rights, however. Rights come, and rights go: different governments introduce new rights, applying to some tenants and not to others, or they may give landlords greater power, and so on. Indeed, *most* changes of government bring about a change in the tenancy laws. The end result is that it is impossible to describe simply and easily the rights of private tenants as a whole. It is necessary, instead, to describe the rights which apply to each different group – indeed, it is the rights which apply which define what the groups are.

Why is it important to find out my class of security?
It is absolutely essential to spend the time finding out what class of security you have. Unless you know what your

class of security is, you will not be able to identify what rights you have in respect of occupation, security, rents, and even repairs and improvements.

It is also important to know your class of security because while some groups have very extensive rights others have very few. For example, protected tenants (see page 52) have both the right to get a fair rent fixed (see Chapter 7) and considerable security of tenure (see Chapter 5). It is, accordingly, relatively safe for them to use the rent powers: they cannot be evicted in retaliation. Assured tenants have less security, but still a lot, and less control over rents, and are unlikely to be subject to eviction because they invoke rent powers.

Tenants and licensees with restricted contracts (see page 70) however, while enjoying the right to have a reasonable rent fixed (see Chapter 6), have only limited security (see Chapter 5). If you have a restricted contract, therefore, and use your rent-fixing rights, you are likely to be faced with retaliatory eviction action.

Whether or not this is a likelihood in your particular case, and whether or not you want to take the risk, is entirely a decision for you; but you have to know what your position is before you can properly decide. The position with other classes of occupation can be even more severe: there may not be limited security so much as no security at all.

What are the classes of security?

The classes of security within the private sector are as follows: protected tenants; protected shorthold tenants; assured tenants; assured shorthold tenants; and restricted contracts. There is a sixth class, inasmuch as some occupiers will not fall into any one of these first five classes, and accordingly are unprotected tenants and licensees. They need no definition; they exist by default – i.e. this 'sixth class' consists of everyone else (not in one of the first five classes). (They do, however, have some, fairly basic, rights – including normally the right not to be evicted without court order: see Chapters 4 and 5.)

How do I find out my class of security?

In order to find out what your class of security is, it is necessary to proceed through the following questions. Start with: 'Am I a protected tenant?' If the answer is, 'Yes', you need go no further. If the answer is, 'No', you will have to ask, in turn: 'Am I a protected shorthold tenant?' (see page 64), 'Am I an assured tenant?' (see page 66), 'Am I an assured shorthold tenant?' (see page 70), 'Do I have a restricted contract?' (see page 70). If you do not fall into any of these five classes, you will be unprotected. (You will still have *some*, fairly basic, rights: see the chapters which follow.)

Am I a protected tenant?

A protected tenant is one who gets the full benefit of the range of rights contained in the Rent Act 1977 and related Acts of Parliament (usually called 'the Rent Acts' for brevity). The starting-point is to assume that *all tenancies granted before 15 January 1989* are within the Rent Acts, unless and until the Acts say otherwise. The best way to approach the matter is to ask first if the letting is *within* protection (on its face), and, secondly, if it is *excluded* for some other reason.

A. Tenancy Within Protection

The first point to emphasize is that full protection under the Rent Acts applies *only* to *tenancies*, i.e. not also to licences (see Chapter 1). Secondly, the Acts apply only to tenancies granted before 15 January 1989: (a) let for residential (i.e. not business) purposes; (b) let for use as one home (not necessarily a whole house, a tenancy of a room or flat will qualify, but not let to one person for the express purpose of use as or subdivision into several different homes); and (c) which does not involve sharing 'living accommodation' with the landlord.

This is not the same as living in the same house as your landlord; nor does it matter if you only share a bathroom or lavatory with your landlord. If you share a kitchen with your landlord or some other room such as a sitting-room or dining-room, however, you will not be protected. Instead, and if your letting began before 15 January 1989, you will normally have a restricted contract (see page 70). There is an important difference, therefore, between the letting of a bedsitting-room, with its own cooking facilities, and the letting of a room, in a house or flat, where kitchen, and perhaps another room, is to be shared.

Where a house was let for *both* residential use, *and* business use – for instance, a house of which the ground-floor front room is a shop – the question which must be asked is what was the predominant purpose of the arrangement? Was the property rented *mainly* in order to run a business from it, in which case it will not be treated as a dwelling (but will get some help from the Landlord and Tenant Act 1954 which deals with business lettings), or *mainly* to live in, in which case a residence?

In one case, a man had a house and from the attic of it ran a Sunday School. A Sunday School could have been considered a 'business' for these purposes, but it was held that it was only an incidental or ancillary use. Similarly, an elderly lady, who found that her house was too big for her, rented out rooms to a few lodgers: as a question of fact, the courts held this was not a 'business', but just 'part of the way she lived'. A doctor rented a house, and set aside one room as an additional 'surgery' but as his main practice was elsewhere, he kept protection. In another case, decided at the same time, a man using a flat as a business *base*, i.e. printed notepaper, telephone, office, as well as a home, was held to be not protected.

B. *Tenancy excluded from protection*

There is a number of cases when a tenancy which would appear to be protected is in fact excluded. Many of these cases, however, will fall within one of the other four classes of security below. The following are the main exclusions, and do not cover special cases such as licenced premises, agricultural lettings or lettings with substantial land, or 'shared ownership' arrangements where the occupier is both renting premises, and partly purchasing them.

(*a*) *Tenancies granted on or after 15 January 1989*: on this date, the Housing Act 1988 came into force and substituted assured tenancies for protected tenancies, in the case of new lettings (see further below). On the face of it, therefore, there can be no new protected tenancies granted on or after that date. Note, however, that I refer to 'new' tenancies, for in some circumstances it is possible to take over someone else's existing protected tenancy, and even if this should occur on or after that date the tenancy will still be protected – see Chapter 6 for when this is possible.

Otherwise, the circumstances when a new protected tenancy can be granted on or after that date are very few indeed. It can happen if a binding contract for the tenancy had been entered into before that date, even though the tenancy itself did not start until afterwards.

It can also happen if you (on your own or as one of a number of joint tenants) had a protected tenancy from a particular landlord (or a person who was one of a number of joint landlords), and you agree to enter into a new tenancy, even of different premises. Part of the purpose of this is to stop landlords tricking their tenants into giving up the much more valuable protected tenancy in favour of an assured tenancy (i.e. a new tenancy, after 15

January 1989), but it is also in part to permit landlords and tenants to agree a change in premises, without the tenant having to give up the more valuable class of tenancy.

Finally, in Chapter 5, we will see that a landlord can obtain a possession order against a protected tenant, from a court, if the court considers it reasonable for the tenant to move to suitable alternative accommodation. On the face of it, your tenancy of the new accommodation will not be protected, because it begins after 15 January 1989, and your old landlord may not be your new landlord – he or she may have arranged for someone else, for example a related company, to give you the tenancy. In such circumstances, you will still be a protected tenant, *if, but only if,* the court which makes the order against you directs that your new tenancy should be protected.

With these exceptions, if your letting began on or after 15 January 1989, you cannot have a protected tenancy, and are likely instead to have an assured tenancy. Unless you fall within one of these exceptions, if your tenancy began on or after that date you should go next to the question 'Am I an assured tenant?' below.

(b) Resident landlords: I have already described one sort of resident landlord whose tenants will be left outside of protection – those who share with them a living-room, or something more than merely a bathroom or lavatory. Commonly, though, landlords live in the same house or flat, without sharing a living-room with their tenants.

A resident landlord cannot be a *company*, because, of course, a company does not 'live' at all. If you have a company landlord, you may skip this heading. Also, a landlord living in another flat in a purpose-built block of flats will not be a resident landlord (although if you live in the *same* flat as your landlord, he or she not only can be but almost certainly will be a resident landlord, even though the block is purpose-built).

To qualify as a 'resident' landlord, the landlord must

actually use some part of the house or flat *as a home*. That is to say, it will not be enough for the landlord to reserve a room for the mere occasional visit, as an office (for rent collection or other business), or just in order to claim to be resident. On the other hand, a landlord can claim to have *two* homes (especially if one is a long way away). It is really a question of common sense whether the way the landlord is using his or her part of the premises makes it capable of being described as 'a residence' or not.

The residence by the landlord must be continuous. This does not mean that he or she has to be there every night, because if that was correct it would not be possible for a landlord to have 'two homes' in the way described. But at all times, it must be possible for the landlord to say, in a common sense way, that the part kept for his or her use is 'a home'. It follows if the landlord rents out that part, other than by way of an informal and temporary licence to, for example, a friend or member of his or her family, continuous residence will have ceased, and you will 'spring' into protection. Once 'in' protection, you stay in.

There are a few exceptions to this general rule. When a landlord dies, the executors have up to two years in which to sell the property, as if the landlord was still alive. They may do this by eviction (see Chapters 4 and 5) or else by selling it to a new resident landlord, i.e. someone who comes in and lives in the deceased landlord's part.

If the landlord does not die but wishes to sell, without evicting you, he or she may sell to a new resident landlord: in this case, a notice must be served by the new landlord on you, within twenty-eight days of the departure of the old landlord, saying that he or she is going to move in. The new landlord then has six months in which to move in, without you becoming protected. There are other provisions governing a landlord who is a trustee for a resident beneficiary.

The rule that there must be continuous residence by

the landlord is otherwise absolute. The trickiest question to answer is *from* when there must be continuous residence. If the tenancy began on or after 14 August 1974 (when a new Rent Act came into force), the answer is simple: the residence must be continuous from the start of the tenancy (subject to the exceptions described).

But you may still be in occupation under a tenancy which began before that date, in a house with a resident landlord. In this case, you have to ask two questions. First, has the landlord been in continuous occupation since that date? If no, you will have become protected for the reason stated above. If yes, you have to go on to the second question. That is: on 13 August 1974 (i.e. immediately before the new Rent Act came into force) were you a protected tenant?

This means we have to go back to the law which operated at that date. You may not have been a protected tenant for any one of a number of reasons set out below. You may not have been a protected tenant because you shared living accommodation with your landlord. Or you may not have been a protected tenant because you had a furnished tenancy.

Whether or not you had a furnished tenancy is itself not a straightforward question to answer. It does not depend on whether *any* amount of furniture was provided, but upon whether the value, to *you*, (but objectively assessed – you cannot simply pick a figure out of thin air!) of the furniture which was provided formed a substantial proportion of the whole rent. (Although this is obviously a difficult formula, it is worth paying some attention to what it means, because a very similar formula will recur in two further places, below – one in connection with protected tenancies, and one in connection with restricted contracts.)

It is important to note that what is in issue is the value to you. The value of furniture provided by the landlord, *to* the landlord, was huge, not in cash terms, but because it kept you out of protection. To you, it is more likely to have been an annoyance than an asset.

The question is approached by valuing the furniture, from the point of view of its use to you, *as at the beginning of your tenancy.* Even if the value was 'negative' (i.e. you would have rather it was not there), *some* value will be attached, although perhaps only nominal. A 'fair' return on this sum will then have to be calculated. 20 per cent is likely to be the top figure: that is the amount which it will be assumed is paid 'out of' the rent towards the furniture. If this amount in turn amounts to less than 10 per cent of the rent, it will be treated as insubstantial. If it amounts to more than 20 per cent, as substantial. At 15 per cent, probably substantial; at 10–15 per cent, a grey area which could go either way.

By way of example, the value of the furniture to you is determined at £500. The 'return' on this may be £75 a year (15 per cent). If your rent at the beginning of your tenancy was £750 (or more) a year, the proportion of your rent attributable to furniture would have been 10 per cent (or less). This would not be substantial. If your rent was only £375 (or less) a year, the proportion would have been 20 per cent (or more), and hence substantial.

In the event, if you were protected on 13 August 1974, then even though your landlord has been in continuous occupation since, he or she will not qualify as a resident landlord and you will not be excluded from protection for this reason; if you were not protected on this date, and the landlord has been in continuous residence since, you will not be protected. Tenants excluded from protection under this heading will normally have 'restricted contracts' (see below).

Note: a wily landlord could use the 'resident landlord' provisions to take away protection from an unsuspecting, already protected tenant. This could be done by moving into the premises, so as to take up residence, and then asking or persuading you to move to a new room, under a new tenancy. The landlord would then say he or she had been resident since the start of *that new* tenancy. Such an arrangement does not work, because there is a specific provision in the Rent Act to deal with it.

(c) *Non-resident landlords*: there is a number of different classes of non-resident landlords. First of all, there are local authorities, housing associations (who are registered with the Housing Corporation or Housing For Wales – a body calling itself a housing association which is not registered with the Housing Corporation or Housing for Wales is just like any other private landlord), charitable housing trusts, housing co-operatives, new town and other (for instance, rural, urban) development corporations, housing action trusts and the Housing Corporation and Housing For Wales themselves. If your landlord is one of these bodies, you will not be protected, and your rights are dealt with in *The Public Tenants Handbook*.

As for the Crown, which owns a lot of residential property, its tenants are protected tenants if, but only if, the property is under the management of a body known as the Crown Estates Commissioners. Most Crown property is under this management, although some is under the management of government departments, and some under direct management. Crown tenants whose property is under the Estates Commissioners' management are protected, but others are not (and will not fall into any of the following classes, nor are public tenants – they are wholly unprotected).

Do not be fooled by other grand-sounding bodies: the British Museum, the Church Commissioners or the like. They are the same as any other private landlord. Companies are a common class of landlord again, like any other private landlord. None of these bodies can be resident landlords, although the tenants could be excluded from protection under one of the headings to follow.

(d) *Protected shorthold, assured and assured shorthold tenancies*: each of these classes of tenancy is described below, under its own heading. If you have one of these terms, you are not a protected tenant (although protected shorthold tenants enjoy a limited number of the rights of the protected tenant (see Chapters 5 and 7).

(e) *High Rateable Value*: a tenancy will not be a protected tenancy if the premises which are the subject of the tenancy have a rateable value of more than £1,500 in Greater London or £750 elsewhere. Rateable value are assessments used by local authorities for the purpose of levying rates. It is extremely unlikely that you will occupy premises of such a high rateable value, for it is only the premises which are the subject of the tenancy which count, not the house or block of which your tenancy may be only a part.

If in doubt, it is up to the landlord to prove that this exemption applies: doubt may arise if there is no separate assessment (i.e. you occupy part only of a house, but the rateable value has not been apportioned) but, again, it is so unlikely that the rateable value will be this high that the possibility may be disregarded until the opposite is shown by the landlord.

(f) *Level of rent*: the Rent Acts were not designed to deal with those who own long leases, and pay a small 'ground rent' each year. They are treated as owner-occupiers and are not covered in this book: see *The Owner–Occupiers Handbook* in this series. The way they are kept out of protection is by excluding those who pay what is called a 'low rent'. This is a rent of less than two thirds of the rateable value of the premises which are the subject of the tenancy (see last heading). This applies, however, whether or not you have a long lease. If, therefore, you pay a rent of less than two thirds of the rateable value of the premises, or you pay no rent at all, you will not be protected, although provided you pay *some* rent (i.e. you do not live rent-free) you may have a restricted contract, see page 70).

There are two observations to make about this provision. First of all, there *are* in fact quite a few people who pay a low rent as defined in this way, but yet who *are* fully protected. These are those tenants who were, until in 1980 the government changed the law, known as 'controlled tenants'.

Controlled tenants paid a very low rent. They are all old tenancies which began before 1957. Most former controlled tenants are elderly. Once they ceased to be controlled tenants, because of the change in the law, the landlord became entitled to increase the rent, to the same level as other fully protected tenants pay (see Chapter 8). However, landlords might not have asked for an increase for a while, or even yet, or the rent increase may have been staggered or the Rent Officer may have fixed a very low rent because many controlled tenancies were notoriously in property of an appallingly low standard. In any of these cases the rent may be less than two thirds of the rateable value, but the tenancy will still be protected.

The other observation relates to 'no rent' cases. Most people paying no rent will nowadays be considered licensees, not tenants (see Chapter 1). But this does not necessarily follow if your accommodation is tied (see Chapter 1). If you are a service tenant (*NB* not a service occupier), you may be paying no rent, or a low rent, because your rent is dealt with along with your wages. On the face of it, this 'level of rent' provision will prevent you being protected.

There are two approaches which have to be distinguished. It may be that there is a fixed amount of rent, which happens to be deducted from your wages. This you may treat as if you are paying rent and, provided that rent is not a low rent, you will still be protected. On the other hand, there may be no fixed amount of rent, just a lower level of wage attributed to the provision of accommodation. This will be treated as if no rent was paid.

(g) *Student lettings*: Lettings by *specified* educational institutions, to their own students or to students attending (or about to attend) *another* specified educational institution, are not protected. 'Specified' means that the educational institution has been included in a list issued by the government. If you have a student letting, you may well have a restricted contract (below).

(h) *Holiday lettings*: a holiday letting is one where the purpose is for you to use the premises in connection with a holiday. Holiday lettings are a popular form of Rent Act evasion, like the non-exclusive occupation agreements described in Chapter 1. They must be considered in exactly the same way: are they genuine, or a 'pretence', or a 'sham' (or 'false label')? If it can be shown that the true agreement was something else, i.e. a normal tenancy, the law will treat it as such, rather than as a holiday letting.

You have to show, therefore, that there were matters known to the landlord (or his or her agents) which were inconsistent with the idea of holiday letting, for instance that you were working or studying. It may be that the landlord asked for a reference, which would have revealed that you were in employment. Even if the landlord was just given your employer's name and did not take up the reference, the point will be well made. Similarly, any other evidence which shows that the landlord knew you were not on holiday – including what was said before or at the time the tenancy was agreed – will be admissible to show that the letting was not genuinely a holiday letting.

If it cannot be shown that the arrangement was phoney, then the letting will be outside Rent Act protection (and also cannot be a restricted contract).

(i) *Personal services*: Some letting arrangements carry

with them additional rights or facilities, which can be called 'personal services'. I use the term 'personal services' to distinguish them from services such as gas, electricity, hot water, cleaning the hall, stairs, bathroom, lavatory or other common parts of a building which is used by more than one household.

Personal services are, rather, such things as doing your laundry, changing the sheets, cleaning the room, and so on. In other words, services which, although they may also be done for other tenants, are in some way 'personal' or 'particular' to you. Having a resident housekeeper on call is partially a personal service to you, but it is also a service which is 'part-and-part' to landlord and to you.

Personal services will only keep you out of protection if their value *to you* forms a substantial proportion of the rent paid. This is exactly the same test as used to apply to deciding whether or not premises were furnished or unfurnished in law (see page 57). The *value* (from your point of view) must be calculated, apportioning appropriately between landlord and you how much value each gets out of those services which are part-and-part of value to each (e.g. resident housekeeper, window cleaning).

It will not be necessary to apply a 'return' on this amount, as with the capital expenditure on furniture, because in this case we are dealing with sums which are paid out regularly by the landlord. Only the part attributable to each tenant is to be counted, though, so that some costs have to be spread proportionately between all the tenants in a house or block of flats. If the amount attributed to each tenant forms a substantial part of the whole rent paid (see above, in relation to furniture), you will not be protected. The question is decided in relation to the services provided, and costs of provision, as at the commencement of tenancy. If you are excluded from protection for this reason, you should have a restricted contract (below).

(j) *Board*: Board means meals. If you are provided with *any* meals by the landlord (not just of a substantial value), your tenancy is not protected. An early morning cup of tea is counted as too small to matter, but breakfast will count as a meal. If the value of the board to you does not form a substantial proportion of your rent (the same test as with personal services, and furniture), you will probably have a restricted contract. Otherwise you are unprotected.

One problem is that of the landlord who provides a box of prepackaged breakfasts by the week (long-life milk, cereal, perhaps eggs, teabags), for you to prepare for yourself. This is probably not board because board implies a degree of preparation of the food by the landlord even if of not much food.

Am I a protected shorthold tenant?

Protected shorthold tenancies were a creation of the Housing Act 1980. They were allegedly designed to 'breathe some life' into the dying private rented sector. They have been a considerable failure, and there are so few of them about that they have made no real impact at all. This is probably because rents, charged under them are still limited by the Rents Acts (see Chapter 8) and landlords preferred to engage in one of those agreements like a 'non-exclusive occupation agreement' or a 'holiday letting', described earlier, which left them free to charge any rent they liked, as well as to evict more or less at will, until the government introduced in 1988 the new classes of assured letting, and shorthold assured letting (below).

The provisions governing protected shorthold tenancies are complex. A protected shorthold tenant is a tenant who would have been a protected tenant, but for the application of a series of conditions. It follows that someone who was excluded from protection for any of the *other* reasons set out above will not be a protected shorthold tenant.

Protected shorthold tenancies can only have been created *after* 28 November 1980 (when the provisions were brought into force), and *before* 15 January 1989. A protected shorthold tenancy granted to someone who was already living in the same premises (the same part of a house or flat) as a protected tenant, i.e. an attempt to trick a tenant out of existing protection, will fail, because the Act specifically deals with this (although not to the same extent as with resident landlords, where protection extends to anyone living in the same house: see page 58).

Protected shorthold tenancies had to be for a fixed term. They must have been for not less than one year and not more than five years. It does not include a periodic tenancy, therefore, such as weekly or monthly, even if it lasts for more than a year, unless such a tenancy has *followed* a fixed-term shorthold, i.e. is an effective continuation of it.

There must be nothing in the tenancy agreement which permits the landlord to give notice to bring the term to an end before the stated date, *except* a provision allowing the landlord to bring it to an end because you fail to pay the rent or break some other term of the tenancy.

In Greater London, there must either have been a rent registered for the premises, or what is known as a certificate of fair rent (a provisional assessment) at the time the tenancy was granted (see further, Chapter 8). This provision does not apply in the rest of the country.

Finally, before the tenancy was granted, the landlord must have given you a notice, in a prescribed form, which sets out basic information, advising you both of what rights you have, and of the fact that the letting is a shorthold, in other words that the landlord will be able to reclaim possession in due course (see Chapter 5).

Although the requirement for prior notice is stated to be an absolute obligation, it may be noted (see Chapter 5) that the courts can, in exceptional circumstances, waive the requirement, i.e. permit a landlord to claim that the letting was a shorthold even if the prescribed form was not given. The court cannot waive any of the other requirements, however, and should only use this power in cases of, for example, a minor technical flaw in the form, and only if it is 'just and equitable' to use its discretion in this way.

Am I an assured tenant?

The term 'assured tenant' was first used, before the Housing Act 1988 applied it more widely, to indicate a very special type of tenancy – initially it referred to tenants of new premises only (built after the introduction of the Housing Act 1980), and then for a very short time (from 1987) both of new premises and those on which a specified amount of money had been spent to improve them. These 'old' assured tenancies will not be described in this book. However, when the Housing Act 1988 came into force, they were 'converted' into assured tenancies as that term came to be used, and as it will be described below.

It is not strictly true, therefore, to say that assured tenancies all began on or after 15 January 1989, when the Housing Act 1988 came into force, but it would be true were it not for this small, exceptional class. Assured tenancies, as that term came to be used from 1988 onwards, are intended to replace protected tenancies under the Rent Act 1977, and to become the principal form of private landlordism. There are many similarities between protected and assured tenancies, and some aspects can be described by cross-reference.

As with the Rent Acts, the starting-point is to assume that *all tenancies beginning on or after 15 January 1989* are assured tenancies, unless and until the Housing Act 1988 says otherwise. The best way to approach the matter is to ask first if the letting is *within* assured protection (on its face), and, secondly, if it is *excluded* for some other reason.

A. *Tenancy within assured protection*

The first point to emphasize is that assured protection applies only to *tenancies*, i.e. not to licences. Secondly, the Act applies only to tenancies (a) let for residential (i.e. not business) purposes, (b) let to a tenant who is an individual, rather than a company (or, if joint tenants, all of whom are individuals), (c) let for use as one home (not necessarily a whole house, a tenancy of a room or flat will qualify, but not if let to one person for the express purpose of use as or subdivision into several different homes), (d) with the tenant (or if joint tenants, at least one of them) using the home as an only or principal home, and (e) which does not involve sharing 'living accommodation' with the landlord.

Both business use and living accommodation have been described above, in relation to protected tenancies. In Chapter 5, below, I will describe the extent of residence which a *protected* tenant needs to keep up, in order to remain a protected tenant. It will be seen that a protected tenant may have two homes, sharing his or her time between each of them. But in the case of an *assured* tenant, the premises must always be used as the tenant's (or one of the joint tenants') *only* home, or at the least his or her *principal* home.

B. *Tenancy excluded from assured protection*

There is a number of cases when a tenancy which would appear to be assured is in fact excluded. In one case, the tenancy may yet fall under the next heading. In other cases, the effect of being excluded from assured protection will be to leave the tenancy wholly unprotected and unassured. The following are the main exclusions, and do not cover special cases such as licensed premises, agricultural lettings or lettings with substantial land.

(a) Tenancy Preceding 15 January 1989: save in the case of the small number of 'old' assured tenancies referred to above, a tenancy which preceded the commencement of the Housing Act 1988 will not be an assured tenancy, but protected, or protected shorthold (above), or restricted or wholly unprotected (below).

In addition, however, if you were a *protected* tenant (not including a protected shorthold tenant), or one of joint protected tenants of the same landlord (or one of joint landlords), the landlord will not be able to 'turn you' into an assured tenant by tricking you into a new tenancy starting on or after 15 January 1989, even if you move by agreement to new premises: the Housing Act 1988 contains provisions to prevent this.

We shall also see in Chapter 5 that the landlord under a protected tenancy may be able to get a court order against you, to move you to 'suitable alternative accommodation'; the new accommodation may be with the same landlord (in which case you will remain protected because of the last paragraph) or with a new landlord, in which case you may still get a protected tenancy if, but only if, the court orders that you should do so in the course of the proceedings.

(b) Resident Landlords: a tenant will not be an assured tenant if his or her landlord is resident. The description that refers to protected tenancies given on page 55 accordingly applies here, save (a) that of course no question of tenancy commencing before 14 August 1974 arises, and (b) that the test of the landlord's 'residence' is not use as *a* home, but use by the landlord as an 'only or principal home'. Otherwise, the same principles apply: the landlord cannot be a company, residence must be continuous, but exceptions are made for sale by landlord, death of landlord

(and where the landlord is a trustee for someone living in the premises).

(c) Non-resident landlords: with one exception, tenants of the same classes of non-resident landlords whose tenants cannot be protected (see page 59) cannot be assured. The exception is that the tenants of registered housing associations and housing trusts are within assured protection, but their particular position is none the less considered – along with the position of the tenants of those other landlords – in the *Public Tenants Handbook* in this series.

(d) Assured shorthold tenants: this class of tenancy is considered below, under its own heading.

(e) High rateable value: the same class of tenant excluded from full protection because of the high rateable value of their premises will also be excluded from assured protection (see page 60).

(f) Level of rent: again, low rent tenancies – as described in relation to protected tenants (see page 60) – are not assured tenancies. There is, of course, no exception for the 'old' controlled tenants whose tenancies preceded the Housing Act 1980. The observations about rent and service tenancies made in relation to protected tenancies do, however, apply also to assured tenancies.

(g) Student lettings: the same exclusion that applied to protected tenancies applies also to assured tenancies (see page 63).

(h) Homeless persons: if you were provided somewhere temporary to live while a local authority determines your application as homeless (see Chapter 2) you are probably a licensee (see Chapter 1). If you are a tenant, you will not normally be an assured tenant for one year from when the authority gives you its decision, unless notified to the contrary *by the landlord,* or the housing is (a) provided *after* the decision, *and* (b) the authority accepts that you have a right to permanent rehousing: see further

The Public Tenants Handbook.

(i) Holiday lettings: the same remarks made in relation to protected tenancies apply also to assured tenancies, including remarks about 'pretences', 'sham' arrangements and 'false labels' (see page 62).

Am I an assured shorthold tenant?

An assured shorthold tenant is an ordinary assured tenant to whom has been granted a fixed-term tenancy (see Chapter 1) for a minimum of six months, and on whom, before the tenancy is entered into, the landlord has served a notice stating that the tenancy is to be an assured short-hold tenancy. If there is *any* power for the landlord to terminate the tenancy (even for breach of a term) within the first six months, the tenancy will not be shorthold. The purpose of shorthold is to provide an additional basis for recovering possession (see Chapters 4 and 5), which in essence is simply that this notice was served.

To prevent trickery, a tenancy which would otherwise be an assured shorthold will not be so if immediately before it started you were the tenant (or one of the joint tenants) of the same landlord under an ordinary assured tenancy, even if under the new tenancy you are only one of a number of (perhaps different) joint tenants, and even if the premises were different. However, if after the initial fixed-term shorthold tenancy comes to an end you stay on in the same premises under an assured tenancy which is not fixed-term, that tenancy will still qualify as shorthold (unless the landlord serves a notice on you saying that it is to be an ordinary assured tenancy.

Do I have a restricted contract?

You may have a restricted contract if your letting began before 15 January 1989 and if you are a tenant, *or* if you are a licensee, provided the relevant conditions are fulfilled. There are two approaches. It is first necessary to ask if you fall *within* the definition of what a restricted contract is; then you have to ask if there is any provision which takes you back out. It is then possible to list those who are within this class.

A. Occupiers within restriction

The conditions for a restricted contract are that (a) the letting began before 15 January 1989, and (b) you pay rent, and (c) you get at least one room that is your own, and (d) you get either services, or furniture, or both, as part of the arrangement for which you are paying.

The requirement that you have one room of your own is not affected if two of you share as joint occupiers, but you will not have a room of your own if you share that room with your landlord, or someone else chosen by your landlord, as happens in a hostel or under a genuine non-exclusive occupation agreement (see Chapter 1). You will still have a restricted contract if you have the minimum one room of your own, even though you also share *other* accommodation with landlord or other occupiers.

In addition, you will have a restricted contract if you are a tenant who has been kept out of protection because you have a resident landlord.

B. Occupiers excluded

If your letting began on or after 15 January 1989 you will not have a restricted contract, as the Housing Act 1988 brought this class of security – for new lettings – to an end. If your landlord is one out of the following classes, you will not have a restricted contract: a local authority, housing action trust, government department, or the Crown (unless the property is under the management of the Crown Estates Commissioners). In addition, the *tenants*, but *not* the *licensees*, of registered housing associations, a charitable housing trust, the Housing Corporation or

Housing for Wales, or a housing co-operative do not have restricted contracts.

Holiday lettings are outside restriction. So also is a letting of premises with a high rateable value (£1,500 in Greater London, £750 elsewhere – see page 60). A letting under which board is provided will be excluded from restriction if the value of the board to you forms a substantial proportion of the rent paid. This is the same formula that was used in relation to defining whether a letting was furnished in law, and whether a tenancy is excluded from protection on account of the provision of services, (see page 57).

C. *Those included*

We may now summarize the list of those who have restricted contracts, as a class, and by reference to the different types of occupation we have already considered. Thus, licensees – none of whom can fall within the first four classes of occupation (protected, protected shorthold, assured and assured shorthold *tenants*) – will be within restriction if they fall within the main definition ((*A*), above) and are not excluded under the last heading ((*B*), above).

In addition, tenants who are excluded from protection because of the provision of services with a value forming a substantial proportion of the rent, tenants excluded from protection because they pay a low rent, and students tenancies (*provided*, in the last two cases, the tenancy includes furniture or services) will have restricted contracts. Tenants receiving board (which is a form of service) will be within restriction, unless excluded on account of its value. Those paying no rent will not have restricted contracts, because payment of rent is one of the conditions defining the class. Finally, and of considerable importance, those who are excluded from full protection (but not assured) because they have resident landlords will have restricted contracts (regardless of furniture or services).

Note that if you have a restricted contract but agree to a major change – e.g. in the room, or in its terms (other than a change in rent to reflect a Rent Tribunal decision: see Chapter 8) – after 15 January 1989, you may be considered to have a new agreement, which is neither a restricted contract nor assured. Do not agree a change without seeking advice first (see Chapter 10).

4: Quitting and Eviction

How long will my tenancy or licence last?

The question of how long a right of occupation will last depends on a number of factors. It is necessary to draw a distinction between the tenancy (or licence) lasting *according to the agreement*, and being allowed to stay on even after the landlord wants you to go because you have rights given by Parliament.

In the first place, your tenancy or licence will last just so long as has been agreed between you and the landlord (which may, however, be an indefinite time, as in the case of a periodic tenancy, i.e. weekly or monthly, or an indeterminate licence, and will be subject to the provisions described below as to how the right may be brought to an end). Only then will it be relevant to ask: does Parliament let me stay on even though my tenancy or licence has come to an end?

Tenancies fall into two classes: periodic tenancies (weekly, four-weekly, monthly, even quarterly or six-monthly – it does not matter which); and fixed-term (which can be for as little as a few weeks, or as much as several years). Licences, too, may be for a specified period, or may be indeterminate. A periodic tenancy continues until it is brought to an end, which is normally by notice to quit; a fixed-term tenancy continues for the period it says, unless it is brought to an end earlier in one of the limited ways this is possible. The position is the same as regards licences, except that there may be less formality about bringing them to an end.

If Parliament has made some provision which permits you to stay on, even though the agreement has come to an end, you will then have security of tenure. Protected tenants (see Chapter 3) have the greatest security of tenure: after the agreement comes to an end, the tenant can simply stay on, and is called a 'statutory tenant', in order to distinguish between staying on under the original tenancy, and staying on under the Act (statute) of Parliament (see Chapter 5). Assured tenants (see Chapter 3) have a similar, but lesser, security (see Chapter 5). Protected and assured shorthold tenants (see Chapter 3) also have some security of tenure (see Chapter 5). Those with restricted contracts, who may be tenant or licensees (see Chapter 3), may get a little security of tenure, either from a Rent Tribunal or from a court (see Chapter 5).

In this chapter, we are concerned with what the agreement says, and how the agreement may be brought to an end, by you or by your landlord, and with what happens then if there is no security of tenure. If there is security of tenure, how much security is available, and how it operates, will be described in Chapter 5.

Can I quit when I want to?

Under a periodic tenancy, you can quit if you want to do so by giving notice to quit at any time and whether or not your landlord is agreeable to your going. You can also quit, when you want, but only if your landlord agrees, by what is called a 'surrender'. Both surrender and notice to quit are described below.

Under a fixed-term tenancy, much will depend on what the agreement says. There may be a clause in the agreement which expressly permits you to quit, perhaps at specific times (for example, after a year), and if there is it will say how you can do so. If there is no such clause in the agreement, you will not be able to quit before the end of the time, unless the landlord agrees, in which case the agreement will be a 'surrender'.

In the case of protected shorthold tenants (see Chapter 3), who will always have a fixed-term agreement to start with, you are entitled to quit by giving one month's notice (if the agreement was for two years or less), or three months' notice (if for more than two years). The notice has to be in writing. You are entitled to do this whether or not your landlord is willing for you to go, and *no matter what it says in the agreement* (Housing Act 1980). Furthermore, if the agreement says that you have to pay the landlord a 'penalty' (i.e. any money) for leaving before the time runs out, that part of the agreement is simply invalid and of no effect.

If you are a licensee (see Chapter 1) with an indefinite licence, that is one which does not state for how long the agreement is to last, you can also give the landlord notice whenever you wish, saying that you intend to go. Provided you give the landlord a sufficient period of warning, (see further below), it does not matter whether or not he or she agrees to your leaving. If, however, the agreement itself says that a minimum period of notice is needed, then you have to give at least as much as the agreement says.

If you are a licensee with a fixed period, then you will only be able to quit before the time runs out if *either* the agreement itself includes a provision enabling you to do so, in which case you must comply with its requirements (for instance, in writing, at a particular point in time, or notice of a specified length), *or* the landlord agrees to your bringing the agreement to an end prematurely.

In *all* cases, *any* occupier who is thinking of leaving before he or she has to, should think hard about whether it is the right thing to do. If you are planning to go to the local authority for help, you are unlikely to get any assistance from it if you have brought your own tenancy or licence to an end, because you will be said to have become 'homeless intentionally', i.e. your homelessness will be your own fault (see Chapter 2). You should only quit somewhere if you are certain you have somewhere else to go to; if you think you have to leave because conditions are so intolerable, try and get some advice before you do anything as to what your position will be afterwards.

Will I have to pay anything if I quit early?

If you quit properly, i.e. in the circumstances described above, you ought not to have to pay anything either in order to quit, or after you have quit (unless, of course, you already owe the landlord money – rent arrears – or have not paid all your bills, such as gas, electricity or telephone).

There is nothing, except in the case of a shorthold tenant, to stop a landlord asking for a payment as a condition of his or her *agreeing* to your leaving, in those cases where his or her agreement is needed. Where his or her agreement is not needed, you will not have to pay. But if a landlord asks for payment in order to agree to your leaving early, it is worth refusing, at least initially, because most private landlords are only too happy to see their tenants and licensees go, and the chances are that it is a 'try-on'.

If you quit improperly, however, by not giving notice, or not getting agreement where that is needed, then the landlord will be able to claim against you for rent during the period the agreement ought to have continued. In the case of a periodic tenant or licensee who merely fails to give notice, that will be for a relatively short period of time, i.e. the period of notice required (although this will be dated from when the landlord finds out, not from when you actually quit). In the case of a fixed-term tenancy or licence, this *could* be for a period as long as the agreement had left to run. It is, however, fairly unusual for a landlord to try and get continuing rent from someone in these circumstances, unless a lot of money is involved, but the possibility cannot be ruled out.

What happens if I end the agreement, but then don't go?

It can happen that you bring an agreement to an end, for example by giving notice to quit a periodic tenancy, because you believe you have somewhere else to go; then that other place falls through and you are stranded. If the landlord is agreeable to your staying on, in effect he or she will simply agree to ignore your notice. However, because private landlords are more commonly pleased to see the back of a tenant or licensee, he or she may not be willing to do this.

In fact, your position will have been worsened, although not necessarily destroyed, by bringing the agreement to an end. One way in which you may be worse off is if you had an agreement for a fixed period, which the landlord has agreed to your surrendering: you are likely to find that you have given up the rest of your time under the agreement and, even if you are then allowed to stay on by law, you will have put yourself in the same position as if you had had a periodic or indefinite agreement which has now come to an end.

There are other ways in which you can be worse off. For example, a protected or a protected shorthold tenant does not have to go if the landlord gives an ordinary notice to quit; the landlord can only evict on one of a limited number of grounds (see Chapter 5). The same is still true if you gave the notice to quit. There will be, however, an additional ground against you, although this will only operate if the landlord has, relying on your notice, already arranged to re-let or sell the premises, *and* it is reasonable to make you go (again, see Chapter 5). This will depend on all the circumstances.

An assured tenant will be in a markedly worse position, because security of tenure as an assured tenant operates differently: broadly, if you give notice to quit or surrender, you will lose your security of tenure, unless the landlord agrees to your withdrawing the notice or surrender. This is so whether you are an assured, or an assured short-hold tenant. Do not say you are quitting, then, unless and until you are absolutely certain.

Those with restricted contracts fall into two classes (see Chapter 5). If your contract began before 28 November 1980 you will still be able to refer your contract to the Rent Tribunal and seek some security, but only if your notice to your landlord has not yet run out by the time you realize you want to stay. Immediate advice should be sought. Those with contracts which began on or after 28 November 1980 have the same theoretical security as if the landlord had given notice, which consists of a period of time given by the court, but it is possible that less time will be given if you are the one who has brought the agreement to an end than otherwise.

Other occupiers are in the same position as if the landlord had brought the agreement to an end. If the landlord has to take court proceedings in order to get you out (see page 94), he or she will still have to do this even though it was you who brought the agreement to an end.

How can the landlord bring the agreement to an end?

We are concerned here with how the landlord can bring the *agreement* to an end, *not* with whether or not the landlord can evict you. The point is that normally the landlord has to bring – or be able to bring – the agreement to an end before he or she can even *seek* to evict you. In the normal case of a periodic tenancy or licence, the landlord can bring the agreement to an end by giving notice (see next question and answer). In the case of an assured or assured shorthold tenancy, however, the process works differently because the landlord cannot bring the agreement to an end at all, *unless* the court will allow him or her to evict. Accordingly, in place of ordinary notice, there are special forms of notice – stating that the land-lord is to seek to evict you. These are also described in the next answer.

If you have a fixed-term tenancy, and unless you are willing to surrender, the landlord normally has to let you stay on until the agreement runs out (and if you have security, even after that – see Chapter 5). In other words, you have 'contractual security' for the period you and the landlord have initially agreed.

However, most fixed-term tenancy agreements contain a provision saying that if you break any of the terms of the agreement – for instance, the agreement to pay rent, not to commit a nuisance to neighbours, not to use the premises for any business purpose – the landlord can 'forfeit' the tenancy, in other words bring it to an end prematurely. Although the language used may be different it is likely that there will be a similar provision in a licence for an agreed period. Remember, however, that we are only concerned here with bringing the agreement to an end: you may still not have to go, and will not usually have to leave without a court order to do so.

It is worth noting that even periodic tenancies, or licences, can contain forfeiture clauses, or their equivalent. This is unusual, but sometimes happens if a landlord has drawn up an agreement himself or herself, or if the agreement is drawn up in an especially intimidatory manner. Because notice is to easy to give to bring a periodic agreement to an end (see below), such clauses do not have much value, and may well be ignored in favour of notice, by the landlord. They are, however, not 'invalid' (save in the case of an assured or assured short-hold tenant) and if used would operate in the same way as for a fixed-term agreement (see below).

What is a notice to quit?
Notice to quit is the normal way in which a periodic

agreement is brought to an end, whether by landlord or tenant. The term 'notice to quit' is often used in connection with both tenancies and licences. Strictly, it should only be used in connection with tenancies, but I shall deal here with the notice bringing both classes of occupation to an end. In addition, under the new 'assured' system, notices to quit are no longer used *by landlords* (they may still be used by you): instead, landlords serve a 'notice of seeking possession' which warns you of impending proceedings to try and evict you, and the grounds for them. I shall also deal with these notices in this answer.

A valid notice to quit must be served to end a periodic tenancy, whenever *you* are seeking to end it, *even if* it is an assured periodic tenancy. Unless or until *you* have served a valid notice to quit, and it has expired, you will be likely to remain liable for the rent (although you will not be so if the landlord relents). The only exception to this is if you reach agreement with the landlord that permits you to 'surrender' your tenancy to him without notice; but if you simply 'abandon' the premises, it will be up to the landlord whether to treat this as an act of surrender, or whether to treat you as still a tenant (and therefore liable for the rent) (see 'What is a surrender?' on page 89).

A valid notice to quit *must* be served *by a landlord* before he or she can seek a possession order against a protected or protected shorthold periodic tenant, or a tenant with a restricted contract, or an unprotected periodic tenant. A valid notice must be served by you or the landlord to bring to an end a periodic licence, whether or not it is a restricted contract. The only circumstance, then, in the case of a periodic arrangement (other than surrender), when notice to quit is *not* needed is when it is replaced by notice of seeking possession of an assured or assured shorthold tenancy.

The difficulty is to identify what constitutes a 'valid' notice in each case. The rules are different for different classes of arrangement. Here, however, not only are we concerned with the difference between assured and assured shorthold tenancies and others, and between tenancy and licence, but also between a new class of distinction: excluded tenancies and licences, and those which are not excluded.

Excluded tenancies and licences

Regardless of class of security (see Chapter 3), a tenancy or licence is an excluded tenancy or licence if one of the following conditions is fulfilled:

1. Under the terms of the arrangement, you share accommodation with the landlord, and both before the arrangement began and at the time it comes to an end the landlord occupies premises as his or her only or principal home (see Chapter 3) of which the shared accommodation forms part. For this purpose, *any* accommodation is 'shared', *other than* a storage area, or a staircase, passage, corridor or other means of access. The definition is *not* the same as when you are sharing 'living accommodation' (see Chapter 3). This sort of case arises, therefore, where you occupy a room in the landlord's house or flat, and share even as little as a bathroom or toilet, or kitchen, with the landlord.

2. Under the terms of the arrangement, you share any accommodation (of the same order as that described above) with a member of the landlord's family, and immediately before the arrangement began and at the time it comes to an end that member of the family occupied premises as his or her only or principal home of which the shared accommodation forms part, *and* immediately before the arrangement began and at the time it comes to an end *the landlord* occupies as his or her only or principal home other premises in the same building. This does not apply if the building is a purpose-built block of flats (see Chapter 3).

In this sort of case, the landlord has divided his or her house into flats, is living in one of them him- or herself, and you are living in another with his or her relative, sharing some accommodation with that relative. But if the building is a purpose-built block of flats, the landlord living in one, and you are sharing with his or her relative in another, you will not have an excluded tenancy or licence for this reason.

3. If you entered somewhere as a squatter (see Chapter 1), but it was agreed that you could stay on for a while, so that for a short period you have become a licensee, or if the landlord persuades you to leave the premises you squatted and move somewhere else for a short while as a licensee, you will be an excluded tenant or licensee where you have been allowed to stay.

4. If you have only been allowed in for a holiday, or if you have an informal arrangement under which you are paying neither rent, nor any other 'consideration' (e.g. performing services for the landlord), i.e. an entirely non-commercial arrangement, you are an excluded tenant or licensee.

5. Occupiers in a hostel owned by *public* landlords are excluded; the Secretary of State can add other people to the list of hostel owners whose occupiers are excluded, which might include some who class otherwise (for the purposes of this book) as private landlords.

Valid notices

We can now turn to examine what constitutes a valid notice to quit for different classes of occupation.

(a) All tenants *other than* excluded tenants whose tenancies began on or after 15 January 1989. (Bear in mind that a *landlord* cannot serve a notice to quit on an assured or assured shorthold tenant: he or she has to serve a notice of seeking possession.) To be valid, a notice to quit a periodic tenancy, other than by or to an excluded tenant whose tenancy began on or after 15 January 1989, must be in writing, and for a minimum of four weeks, or a period of the tenancy, whichever is the longer (Protection From Eviction Act 1977). Thus, four weeks is enough for a weekly tenancy, but a full month is needed for a monthly tenancy. The notice has to identify landlord, tenant and premises in question. It also has to identify the date on which it is to expire. This date must be either the first or the last day of a period of the tenancy; for example, notice to quit a weekly tenancy which commmences on a Friday must expire on a Thursday or Friday.

To get around this technicality, and because it is often difficult to recall exactly what is the correct day of commencement of a tenancy (although, in the absence of any other proof, the rent-day will be assumed to be the first day of each period of the tenancy), notices to quit often contain what is called a 'saving clause'. What happens is that a date is stated in the notice, which is believed to be one of the two correct dates (first or last day of a period), and the notice then continues: '. . . or at the end of the period of your tenancy expiring upon the . . .'. In effect, this throws the burden of identifying the date on which the notice expires back on to the person it is given to.

What has been said this far is as true of notices to quit served by tenants as it is of notices served by landlords. A notice served by a landlord, however, has to go further. It has to give the tenant certain information as to rights. That information is:

1. If the tenant or licensee does not leave the dwelling, the landlord or licensor must get an order for possession from the court before the tenant or licensee can lawfully be evicted. The landlord or licensor cannot apply for such an order before the notice to quit or notice to determine has run out.

2. A tenant or licensee who does not know if he has any

right to remain in possession after a notice to quit or a notice to determine runs out can obtain advice from a solicitor. Help with all or part of the cost of legal advice and assistance may be available under the Legal Aid Scheme. He should also be able to obtain information from a Citizens' Advice Bureau, a Housing Aid Centre or a rent officer.

What this notice means is that you do *not* have to go unless a court orders you to do so. In any event, you should take advice in one of the ways mentioned. If a notice to quit does not have this information with it, the notice to quit is quite simply not worth the paper it is written on: it is invalid. However, it is probably valid enough if the information is given on an attached piece of paper, and perhaps even in a covering letter: the exact same words do not have to be used, although substantially the same information must be given.

In addition to the validity of the notice to quit, the notice must be validly served. This normally means that it is served in person, although of course this can be done by post. A notice to quit is not validly served just by leaving it at the premises, although it probably is validly served if it is given to someone who could be described as 'acting' for the landlord or the tenant, such as an employee of the landlord, the tenant's spouse, or, if the tenant is away, someone left in charge of the premises by the tenant.

(b) Excluded tenants, whose tenancies began on or after 15 January 1989. In the case of such a tenant, the formalities are very few indeed. Whether given by you or the landlord, the notice to quit does *not* have to be in writing (though it is always preferable that it should be so), and need only be of one period of the tenancy. If *you* are giving notice to quit, you are well advised to put it in writing, because you may wish to use the 'saving clause' described above to ensure that it is valid.

(c) All licences, *other than* an excluded licence. Since

15 January 1989, it has been a requirement that notice to a licensee – even if the licence began before that date – must be in writing, for a minimum period of four weeks, and contain such information which will be prescribed by law. There is not the technicality as to date of expiry of notice that applies in the case of a tenant, nor need the notice necessarily expire on the same day as the beginning or end of a period of the licence, although whether or not the landlord can terminate the arrangement in the middle of such a period depends on the terms of the agreement itself. It is also possible that the agreement itself might require a longer period of notice than four weeks, and if it does so then the longer period will apply, e.g. one month. The information is the same as under (a), above.

(d) Excluded licences. Unless the agreement itself makes provision for the way in which notice is to be given, or a minimum period, in which case what the agreement says will prevail, the notice can be oral, and has to be for no more than a 'reasonable' period. 'Reasonable' varies from letting to letting, and everything has to be taken into account: length of time you have been in residence, availability of other accommodation, cause of bringing the agreement to an end (for example, bad behaviour), separateness or closeness of shared living accommodation. If the arrangement is one that has gone on for some months, and there was no reason to expect it to come to an end at a particular time, several weeks may be considered reasonable.

Notice of seeking possession

A landlord cannot serve notice to quit to bring to an end a periodic assured or assured shorthold tenancy. (Although an assured shorthold tenancy has to be for an initial fixed term, unless some other agreement is reached between you and the landlord it will automatically be followed by an assured periodic tenancy, which remains shorthold in practice, even if not in name: see Chapters 3 and 5.) Instead, notice of seeking possession has to be served, which has to be valid. The requirements are different for an ordinary assured periodic tenancy, and one which follows an assured shorthold fixed term and which may therefore be considered an assured shorthold periodic tenancy, but in either case the actual agreement does not come to an end until the date specified by the court, pursuant to proceedings, for the tenant to quit.

1. *Assured tenancy.* Before seeking an order for possession against an assured tenant (whether periodic or fixed-term) the landlord – or if there are joint landlords, at least one of them – must serve a notice of seeking possession on the tenant, *unless* the court decides that it is 'just and equitable' to proceed without such a notice, e.g. if the reason for the eviction is very serious indeed, and you can have been in no doubt but that such proceedings were immediately to be brought.

The notice must be in the form prescribed for this purpose. The notice has to specify what 'grounds for possession' are alleged: see Chapter 5, page 123). The court can, however, give permission for the landlord later to add to or alter these grounds. The purpose of warning you of the grounds is to give you an opportunity to rectify any wrong, e.g. non-payment of rent, so that the notice ought to say more than 'rent arrears' or 'nuisance', but specify how much you are in arrears or to whom you have been a nuisance.

The notice has to tell you of the *earliest* date when the proceedings might be begun. The minimum period is at least two weeks from the date on which you are served with this notice, but (a) it cannot be earlier than the date on which your tenancy could have been terminated by notice to quit (see above), which will normally mean four weeks, and (b) has to be a minimum of two months if the ground on which possession is sought is one of the following (see Chapter 5, page 125): notice of landlord's past or future residence; required by mortgage company; held for minister of religion; demolition, reconstruction or substantial works; tenancy inherited *other than* under statutory succession; suitable alternative accommodation; previous employment with landlord.

The court has no power to waive the requirement for notice, on the grounds that it would be just and equitable to do so, if the ground for possession relied on is the *mandatory* ground of a quarter's rent arrears (see further Chapter 5). The notice also has to tell you that proceedings will be commenced within one year of it being served on you. If the proceedings are not commenced within that year, the notice lapses and a new notice would be needed before the landlord could seek to evict you.

2. *Assured shorthold tenancy.* An assured shorthold tenant may be evicted in the same way as an ordinary assured tenant. *In addition*, the landlord may seek to evict purely because the assured tenancy is shorthold, by a notice which simply states that – no earlier than two months after it has been served – the landlord requires the tenant to go. If the tenancy has become periodic, the two month period must end on the last day of a period of the tenancy, and must be no earlier than the tenancy could have been brought to an end by notice to quit (see above), which will normally not conflict with the two month requirement, but might do so, for example, in the case of a periodic *quarterly* tenancy.

What happens if there are joint tenants?

One joint tenant can serve notice to quit a periodic tenancy (not a fixed-term) *without the consent of the other or others*, which is just as effective as if all the joint tenants had signed it. This means that one joint tenant can take action extremely harmful to others. If there is security, this will follow in the same way and to the same extent as described above, in relation to people who bring an agreement to an end but then change their minds and want to stay on, i.e. a protected or protected shorthold tenant *may* still have security, but an assured or assured shorthold will *not.* The same position is probably true of 'joint licensees'.

If a notice to quit (i.e. a tenancy) is served by the landlord, all the joint tenants have to be named in the notice, but it need only be served on one of you.

What happens if there are joint landlords?

The same is true as for joint tenants: one of the landlords can serve notice to quit, and it is the same as if served by all of them, although all of them must be named in the notice to quit. Similarly, service by you on one of the joint landlords is valid service (see above).

What is a surrender?

A periodic or fixed-term tenancy may be surrendered, but only by agreement. A periodic (i.e. indefinite) or fixed-term licence may also be brought to an end by agreement, but unless the agreement itself requires some specific formality (for example, in writing, time and so on), this is without any of the formality which applies to the surrender of a tenancy.

Strictly, surrender should be by deed, which means a signed and sealed written document. Commonly this does not happen. Before entering into such a deed, you should be absolutely and unequivocally certain that you intend to go and want to get rid of the tenancy.

If there is no surrender by deed, then the law will imply a surrender when you and the landlord are agreed that you are to quit, and you actually do so. If you have agreed and not yet quit, you or the landlord *may* still be held to your word, if, but only if, the one who does *not* want to change his or her mind has in some way acted to his or her detriment on the promise of surrender to come – for example, if you do not wish to change your mind but the landlord does, because you have already taken another tenancy, or if you wish to change your mind but the landlord does not, because he or she has already granted another tenancy or agreed to sell the premises.

Landlords sometimes claim that a tenant has surrendered, because the tenant has gone away for a while, perhaps omitting to pay rent for a period. The courts will not uphold this if you have left someone in occupation, or if your belongings are still there and so on. Indeed, any evidence from you which is accepted by a court as showing that you had not agreed to quit will mean that there has been no implied surrender, because it is at the heart of surrender that there should be an *agreement* to bring the tenancy to an end. If your landlord is claiming that you have surrendered, you should take immediate advice.

Note that, unlike in the case of notice to quit, one joint tenant cannot surrender without the agreement of the other or others: this, again, is because 'mutual agreement' is at the heart of surrender – one (or more) of the parties (i.e. the non-consenting joint tenant) will not be in agreement, and so there can be no surrender.

What is forfeiture?

Forfeiture is the normal way a landlord brings to an end a fixed-term tenancy before its time has run out, and when you do not agree to go; it is only available if the agreement contains a provision permitting him or her to forfeit, which will normally be for breach of a term of the tenancy. You cannot forfeit the tenancy for breach of a term by the landlord. Forfeiture is not a correct term to use in relation to licences, although some fixed-term licences may use the expression and most are likely to contain some equivalent entitlement. In the case of a licence, the only formalities, however, will be those contained in the agreement, not those described here in relation to tenancies.

With one, major, exception, forfeiture must be preceded by a notice, giving the tenant the opportunity to 'rectify' or 'remedy' the breach in question. This is not so, however, in the case of forfeiture for rent arrears. However, whether or not there has been a prior notice, a landlord can only forfeit by order of a court, and in all cases where forfeiture is available, the court has power to grant 'relief' from forfeiture, i.e. to permit you to stay on, although almost certainly on terms that you remedy the breach, such as that you pay off any rent arrears, stop committing a nuisance or doing something else which, under the terms of the agreement, is prohibited.

While forfeiture proceedings are strictly a separate matter from other court proceedings for eviction – for example, for an order against a protected or assured tenant (see Chapter 5) – they will normally be brought at the same time, so that the court will consider the basic question of whether or not you are to be permitted to remain despite your breach of a term of tenancy, under all the different headings which apply: relief from forfeiture, whether or not an order ought to be made against a protected tenant, how much time to allow, and so on (see Chapter 5).

In the case of an assured or assured shorthold fixed-term tenancy, the landlord *cannot* forfeit, and therefore you cannot seek relief from forfeiture. However, if (but only if) there is a forfeiture clause covering the grounds in question, he can achieve the same effect by serving a notice of seeking possession, fulfilling the requirements described above (see page 87) in relation to periodic assured and assured shorthold tenants, with the exception that there is no 'alternative minimum period' based on the earliest date when the tenancy could have been brought to an end by notice to quit (as notice to quit does not apply to fixed-term tenancies). This is only so where the ground on which the landlord seeks possession (see page 123) is one of the following: of the mandatory grounds, required for sale under mortgage, and one quarter's rent arrears; any of the discretionary grounds *except* suitable alternative accommodation, and former employment. In any other case, the landlord must await the end of the fixed-term.

What happens to sub-tenants and licensees if my own right of occupation comes to an end?

In the case of any licensees you may have, their rights to stay in occupation will begin and end with yours. In the case of sub-tenants, a lot depends on *how* your tenancy has come to an end, and on other factors. The 'normal' rule is that if your tenancy comes to an end, any sub-tenancy you have granted also, and automatically, comes to an end. However, there are two exceptions: (i) if *you* are a protected or assured tenant, and your sub-tenant is (or has become) a *legal* (see Chapter 1) *and protected or assured* tenant (which would be somewhat unusual, because if you are living in the same house or flat as your own sub-tenant, you will be his or her 'resident landlord' – see Chapter 3), your sub-tenant will become your landlord's tenant direct if you leave; or (ii) if you surrender or give notice to quit.

This second exception is not well known. It derives from old law which is, however, still valid. It does not apply if your landlord gives you notice to quit. It only applies if you give the landlord a valid notice to quit, or if you and the landlord agree (whether by deed, or by implication) on a surrender. In either of these cases, your sub-tenant will become the tenant of the landlord directly, whether the sub-tenancy is legal or illegal (see Chapter 1). By accepting your notice to quit, or by agreeing to your surrender, the landlord is said to have waived any breach which might have made your sub-tenant an illegal sub-tenant, and has stepped into your shoes (remembering

that you could not take advantage of your own illegality –
see Chapter 1). This will *not* apply if you are a protected
tenant, whose tenancy is already statutory, i.e. the
contract has been brought to an end and you have been
relying on your Rent Act right to remain (see Chapter 5).

What happens if I am living with a tenant who goes?

If you are a licensee, then your right of occupation will
come to an end. If you are a sub-tenant, it will again
depend on what sort of sub-tenancy you have, and the
circumstances in which your landlord (the tenant) goes. If
he or she was a protected or assured tenant, and you are
his or her *legal* (see Chapter 1) *and protected or assured*
sub-tenant, you will become the tenant of the landlord
direct.

This provision will also operate if your landlord, the
tenant, was not an assured tenant, and if your landlord was
not a protected tenant, but in this latter case only because he
or she was tenant of a whole house not let as one dwelling
unit (a house let for subletting), or was on a tenancy at a low
rent for twenty-one years or more.

The provision operates whether the tenant quits by
giving (or being given) notice, or surrenders, or his or her
lease is forfeit, or the tenant dies. However, if the landlord gets a court order to make the tenant go (which he or
she will have to do to bring the tenancy to an end by
forfeiture, and in any event will have to do if the tenant is
unwilling to go, because we are concerned here mainly
with *protected* and *assured* tenancies), any ground for
possession against the tenant (see Chapter 5), such as that
the tenant has been a nuisance or annoyance to adjoining
occupiers, becomes a ground for possession against you too.

That does not mean that if he or she has to go, you will
have to do so as well, because the landlord may have to
show that it is reasonable to evict each of you, and while it
may be reasonable to make the tenant go, it may not be

reasonable to make you do so (see Chapter 5).

If the landlord seeks an order for forfeiture of the tenancy, then you, as a sub-tenant, whether legal or illegal, are entitled to ask the court to grant *you* relief (see above), whether or not the court is willing to grant the tenant relief. If the court is willing to do so, it can make you into the landlord's tenant directly.

You can also become the landlord's tenant directly, whether or not you have or the tenant has a protected or assured tenancy, if the tenant has given a valid notice to quit to the landlord, or if the tenant surrenders (see last question). This will again not be so if the tenant was a protected tenant whose tenancy had already become statutory.

Does the landlord have to get a court order before I have to leave?

Normally, yes. Whatever kind of tenancy you have, the landlord has to get an order before you can be made to go (Protection From Eviction Act 1977). This is also true if you are a service occupier, i.e. licensee in tied accommodation (see Chapter 1). It is also true if you are a licensee who has had a restricted contract (unless that contract started before 28 November 1980 – see Chapter 5).

It is again true if you are or have been a sub-tenant, whether legal or illegal, or a licensee of a tenant, *except*, by a legal 'quirk', if you are or have been the licensee of a *statutory* tenant who has left (i.e. a protected tenant whose tenancy has come to an end – see Chapter 5).

The landlord will *not* need to get a court order against you, however, if you are an excluded tenant whose tenancy began on or after 15 January, 1989, or if you have an excluded licence (whenever it began). These terms are the same as those described above, in relation to notices to quit. However, in the exceptional case of an excluded licence which is *also* a restricted contract which was entered into on or after 28 November 1980 (when the Housing Act 1980 came into force), court proceedings are still required.

If the landlord, or anyone else for that matter, including someone acting on behalf of the landlord, evicts without a court order when a court order is needed, a criminal offence has been committed. The offence is committed whether the eviction is from the whole of the premises or from any part of them. This means that preventing access, shutting you out, throwing you out, blocking up the premises or (and this is not unknown) demolishing the premises, without first getting an eviction order, is illegal. Offences of this order should be reported to the local authority's Tenancy Relations or Harassment Officer. In addition, you will normally be able to take civil action against your landlord, for an illegal eviction.

The advantage of civil action over complaint to the local authority's officer is that if the landlord is not capable of being persuaded to let you back in, an immediate order for your readmittance, and preventing any recurrence of the illegal eviction, will be available from the civil courts, which will not be available from the criminal courts. In addition, you are much more likely to be able to get compensation, for any costs you have run up while out (for instance costs of hotel or eating out, or property damaged during the eviction) and for the hardship it has caused you.

When can the landlord get a court order against me?

Save in the case of an assured or assured shorthold tenant, a court will not make an order against you until after your tenancy or licence has come to an end: until then, you have the right of agreement (even if the landlord has been trying to bring it to an end) to stay in occupation. In the case of tenancy, save one that is assured or assured shorthold, the landlord cannot even *start* the proceedings to get you out until *after* the tenancy has actually come to an end, that is to say after time has run out including the period of the notice to quit.

In the case of a licence, the landlord can start the proceedings before it runs out, but the court will not make an order until after it has run out. (In particular circumstances, landlords can sometimes use proceedings designed for squatters – see Chapter 1 – against licensees: these proceedings are known as 'Order 24' proceedings – see page 101. If the landlord uses them, he or she cannot start them until after even a licence has run out. They are not available against former tenants of any kind.)

Just because the agreement has been brought to an end, or because in the case of an assured or assured shorthold tenant a valid notice of seeking possession has been served, does not mean that the court *will* make an order against you. Protected and assured tenants have considerable security of tenure, and the landlord may very well *not* be able to get an order (see Chapter 5). In the case of protected and assured shorthold tenants, while the landlord will normally be able to get an order against you, he or she may well not have complied with the various technical requirements described above.

Will the court give me time to go?

If you have a protected, protected shorthold, assured or assured shorthold tenancy, or a restricted contract, the powers of the court are closely connected to your security of tenure, and are described in Chapter 5. In most of these cases, some time will be available. Otherwise the court will normally give you no more than two weeks to go, but in cases of exceptional hardship has power to grant up to six weeks (Housing Act 1980). Once the time allowed by the court has run out, most landlords will use the services of the court bailiff to carry out an actual eviction, which may give a little more time (you will be sent a warning notice by the bailiff).

Can the landlord harass me to make me leave?

No. If you are still occupying under an agreement – of any class – *and* if you fall into the category of those people the landlord has to get a court order against before he or she can evict (see above), you fall within the laws against harassment (Protection From Eviction Act 1977). These laws last as long as the right to remain in the premises last, i.e. until the date set by a court for you to leave.

Harassment means doing something which is intended to interfere with your peace and comfort, or that of members of your household (which probably means sharers as well as family), either in order to make you quit, or else to make you stop using some other right (for example your right to a Rent Officer or Tribunal – see Chapter 8 – or to complain about disrepair – see Chapter 9). It is also harassment to withdraw or withhold services, such as gas, electricity, water, telephone if any, with either of the same intentions: to make you quit, or give up some right or other. It is also harassment to do something which interferes with your use of the premises or withdraws services, if the landlord actually knows, or has reason to believe, that it is likely to make you quit or give up some right or other, even if it cannot be proved that this was his or her intention. Offences of this order should be reported to the local authority's Tenancy Relations or Harassment Officer.

Further examples of harassment include: preventing you using some part of the premises which have been let to you (for instance, by cutting off access to one room separate from others), or from using shared facilities such as a bathroom or toilet or a telephone if one is provided, perhaps a coinbox in the common parts; removing furniture or, for example, a fridge or a cooker; pushing you or a member of your family around; standing outside, or next door, or nearby, making a noise; leaving rubbish in or near a property for longer or in greater quantities than usual, so that it smells and becomes a health hazard; intimidating you; even a long and unfounded course of conduct consisting of letters threatening eviction, banging at the door and shouting at an occupier.

In addition, you will be able to take civil action against your landlord if he harasses you. Both tenancies and licences contain provisions which are intended to prevent interference with your right to enjoy the premises. There is a number of 'heads' under which you may sue, and using civil proceedings as well as or instead of complaint to the local authority has the same advantages as with illegal evidence, i.e. being able to get an almost immediate order from the court, and compensation.

Will my landlord sell me my home?

He or she does not normally have to. The 'right to buy', of which you may have heard, applies only in the public sector (see *The Public Tenants Handbook*) or to those holding long leases of houses (not flats), who are treated as owner–occupiers (see Introduction). In addition, there is a new right – called the 'right of first refusal' – under the Landlord and Tenant Act 1987, which may in some circumstances allow protected tenants of flats (but not assured tenants) to join with other residents of the block (whether or not they are also protected tenants, or have some greater right of occupation, e.g. a long lease) to make a 'first bid' if the landlord declares his or her wish to sell. These provisions are extremely complex and cannot be described here, and in all cases will require the assistance of a lawyer (and of a surveyor or valuer): they are described in *The Owner–Occupiers Handbook* in this series.

Sometimes, however, a landlord is willing to sell voluntarily. He or she may approach you and ask if you want to buy. What you pay depends on what the property is worth *to you*, just as it does when deciding to buy a property – or anything else! – on the open market, but if you are a protected or assured tenant the property is a lot less valuable to the landlord than if you are not a protected or assured tenant, or there is no tenant at all. There are no rules about what sort of discount a landlord will give you if he or she wants to sell and you want to buy, but you should look for a reduction of 40 per cent–60 per cent off the market value as it would be if the property was empty.

Certainly, it is worth your while to get your own valuation of the property; you should also have the property surveyed: you may be buying more problems than you realize; for example, serious disrepair, which if you had remained a tenant the landlord would usually have had to pay for (see Chapter 9). You should *always* take advice if possible, and *always* have a solicitor act for you in the transaction. He or she ought to be able to find out if, for example, there is some ulterior and hidden motive on the landlord's part which detrimentally affects the value of the property, e.g. impending local authority action to close the premises (see Chapter 9).

If you approach the landlord asking to buy, he or she may also be willing to sell, but as a matter of common sense the fact that you will have shown your eagerness to buy before he or she has shown his or her eagerness to sell will mean that you are likely to get less of a discount than if he or she approaches you first. It may be, for example, that if you approach the landlord you are only able to agree a reduction of 40 per cent reflecting your tenancy, while if the landlord approaches you it is easier to hold out for 60 per cent. But in either case, these figures are merely examples: you might get even more than 60 per cent if the landlord is very keen to get rid of the property.

Even if you are not a protected or assured tenant, you should get *something*, reflecting not so much the rent you have been paying, but the fact that the landlord will not need to go to the bother of evicting you before putting the property on the market empty. But, of course, your bargaining position for a discount is much weaker than if you had a protected or assured tenancy when, by and large, the landlord is unable to evict you (or else would have to find you other accommodation: see Chapter 5).

Is a court order needed to evict a trespasser?

In general, an owner does not *need* to get a court order before evicting a trespasser. However, an owner who evicts without a court order runs the serious risk of committing a criminal offence under the Criminal Law Act 1977. In some circumstances, though, trespassers too can commit criminal offences under this Act, even if the owner has *not* obtained a court order first.

The offence which an owner seeking to get rid of a trespasser may commit is that of violent eviction. An owner cannot use or threaten violence towards people or property in order to gain entry to premises. This is only so, however, if the person trying to get in knows that there is someone inside the premises *at the time* who is opposing his or her entry. This means that eviction while all the trepassers are out (say at work) will not be illegal. Of course, this provision does not apply to a bailiff acting under a court order.

Furthermore, it is not an offence, provided no more than reasonable and necessary force is used, if the person trying to get in is, or is acting on behalf of, a 'displaced residential occupier'. This means someone who was using the premises as a residence immediately before the trespass, for example a person who has left his or her home empty and returns to find it squatted (this is a very uncommon occurrence).

To facilitate the eviction of trepassers by court proceedings, a special procedure (known as 'Order 24' if it is brought in the county court, and 'Order 113' in the High Court) exists which permits owners to obtain an order in a very short time indeed, and even against 'persons unknown', if he or she is unable to identify the trespassers. If these procedures have been used, or indeed if they could have been (but for some reason or other the owner has used conventional possession proceedings, which take much longer to be heard), the trespasser will commit an offence if he or she resists or intentionally obstructs an officer of the court, such as a bailiff, who is trying to 'execute it', i.e. carry out the eviction.

In addition, a trespasser will commit an offence if he or she fails to leave premises when asked to do so *either* by a displaced residential occupier (above) *or* by a 'protected intending occupier'. This latter phrase means someone either who owns the premises and is intending to live in them, or who is the prospective tenant of the premises, and the landlord is one of the public-sector landlords whose tenants are excluded from Rent Act protection (see Chapter 3).

The offence is failure to leave when asked to do so: the request to the trespasser need not be in writing, but protected intending occupiers have to produce a statement, which will have to be in writing and which proves their status as owner or allocated tenant. It is a defence to a charge under this provision either that the trespasser did not believe that the person trying to evict him or her was a protected intending occupier, or that no statement was produced.

5: Security of Tenure

What does 'security of tenure' mean?

Security of tenure refers to the rights to remain in occupation which have been created by Parliament. These rights are *additional* to those which may have been granted under the agreement of tenancy or licence and, as a general rule, the first place to look is to the contract, and only when the contract has come to an end or notice of seeking possession has been served on an assured or assured shorthold tenant (see Chapter 4) will it be necessary (and highly desirable) to start to consider what further rights are available. Where the Act of Parliament gives you greater rights than the contract however the Act will 'normally' override the contract.

Who has security of tenure?

The main security is that provided to protected tenants, under the Rent Act 1977 and to assured tenants under the Housing Act 1988. The *principal* point of distinction is that the 1977 Act – where it applies – relates mainly to lettings preceding 15 January 1989 while the 1988 Act deals with later lettings. Protected shorthold tenants have some security, under both the Rent Act 1977 and the Housing Act 1980, while assured shorthold tenants have their limited security under the Housing Act 1988. Those with restricted contracts have some, but not much, security under the Rent Acts. The first thing to do, then, is to establish which, if any, of these classes you belong to (see Chapter 3). The second thing to do is to see if your contract has been brought to an end properly or notice of seeking possession has been properly issued (see Chapter 4).

What security does a protected tenant have?

If you are a protected tenant, you can continue to live in your premises for the rest of your life, *provided* you remain a protected tenant, and *unless* the landlord gets an order for your eviction. Furthermore, a member of your family may be able to take over the tenancy from you on your death (see Chapter 6).

A. *Is tenancy still protected?*

There is a small number of circumstances in which a tenancy which has been protected may not be so by the time the tenancy agreement has been brought to an end (see Chapter 4), or may cease to be protected at some point in time after it has come to an end, other than by order of the court.

(a) Change of landlord. It may be that the landlord has sold the premises, or his or her interest in them, to another landlord, and for that reason the tenancy has ceased to be a protected tenancy: for example, if the landlord has become one of the public landlords mentioned in Chapter 3, whose tenants are not protected. A sale to a resident landlord will not cause what has been a protected tenancy to cease to be one (because there will not have been a resident landlord *continuously* since the beginning of the tenancy – see Chapter 3).

(b) Public health. Chapter 9 describes certain types of action which a local authority can take, to stop unfit premises being used for human habitation. If the local authority takes any of these actions, the tenancy will cease to be protected for the purposes of security of tenure. Chapter 6 refers to overcrowding: when premises are illegally overcrowded, then again the tenancy will cease to be protected for the purposes of security of tenure. In each of these circumstances, however, you will almost certainly be rehoused by the local authority.

(c) Use of premises. Chapter 3 described how a tenancy

which was predominantly for a business purpose would not be a protected tenancy. If the use of premises changes from one that is predominantly residential to one that is predominantly business (bearing in mind the meaning of that term – see the example of the Sunday School on page 53), you will cease to be a protected tenant.

(d) Non-use of premises. This is the most important and most common reason why a tenancy which has been a protected tenancy ceases to be one, without a court order.

In Chapter 4, I drew a distinction between the contractual part (or time) of a protected tenancy, and the time following the ending of the contract of tenancy, when you are allowed to remain indefinitely under the Rent Acts, as a 'statutory tenant'. A statutory tenancy, then, starts when the contract of tenancy has been brought properly to an end.

This may be in one of the ways described in Chapter 4. In addition, in Chapter 8, I will describe circumstances in which a landlord can put up the rent; one of the ways used is a 'notice of increase' of rent. If a notice of increase is served while a protected tenancy is still a contractual tenancy, and the rent increase is stated in the notice as not to take effect until after a date when a notice to quit could have taken effect (i.e. at least four weeks, or more if a tenancy is of longer periods, such as monthly), the notice of increase operates *as if* it had been a notice to quit, and accordingly the tenancy becomes statutory.

A statutory tenancy lasts only so long as you (or, if there is a joint tenancy, one of you) are still using the premises *as a home*. When you are no longer doing so, the statutory tenancy comes to an end and you have ceased to be a protected tenant. The same does not apply while the tenancy is contractual: you have rented the premises and you may use them or not as *you* please, not, as it were, as Parliament or the law may please. (However, the fact that you are not living in the premises, enough to count as 'use as a home', during the contractual tenancy may be used as evidence to show that you are not doing so after the tenancy comes to an end.)

The law recognizes that to use premises as a home does not mean that you have to sleep in them every night, or even every week. You may have to go away, perhaps for a very long period. Or you may have to go into hospital, or to go and look after an elderly relative. You might even have two homes: perhaps you have been saving up for retirement and bought somewhere else to live; you are now semi-retired, and live part of the time in one house (the rented house) and part of the time in another.

Absences such as these do not cause the loss of protection. If you are away long enough to raise an inference of a more serious absence (certainly a matter of months rather than weeks), you will still retain your protection if you can show: (a) that you intend to return to use the premises as a home, and (b) that you have left 'signs' of your continued intention to return – furniture, books, other belongings – or else someone to take care of the premises for you, such as a friend or relative.

Indeed, you can even show your intention to retain the premises as your home through a short subletting. But the intention must be a genuine intention to use the premises as a home, not a question of merely keeping your options open, or keeping the premises as an occasional 'convenience'. Both features must be present – intention to return, and some tangible sign of that intention. It is not enough, for example, to leave your child in occupation, if you have no intention to come back there to live yourself.

The rules governing when there is sufficient residence – sometimes called 'statutory residence' – to keep a statutory tenancy alive are *exactly* the same as the rules which apply to determining whether or not a resident landlord (or someone who claims to be a resident landlord) really is in residence, or is merely claiming to live in a bit of a house, just in order to keep his or her tenants out of protection (see Chapter 3). You might be claiming residence just to 'hang on' to a place you don't truly use as a home any more.

One point which emerges from the requirement of use as a home is that if the tenant is not a 'person' but is an 'artificial body', such as a limited company, the tenant cannot 'reside' at all, because companies do not 'live' and have 'homes'. The importance of this is that some landlords try to arrange lettings so that the tenant is not the person who is going to live in the premises but a limited company. The limited company then 'permits' the occupier to live in the property, not as a sub-tenant but as the company's licensee. When the contractual tenancy comes or is brought to an end (and these arrangements are usually fixed term), there is no tenant to become a statutory tenant.

This is a device used like non-exclusive occupation agreements (see Chapter 1) or holiday lettings (see Chapter 3) to try and get round the Rent Act. The question whether or not it will work is decided in exactly the same way as are those 'devices'. Was the arrangement a genuine arrangement, or can the occupier show that it was a 'pretence', 'sham' or 'false label'?

If it can be shown that the company did not really exist, that the landlord insisted that it was formed and/or that the occupiers became a director of it, and that it was always clear and intended that in all other respects it should be a perfectly normal letting, only dressed up in this way in order to try and persuade the court that the tenant is the notional company, it may be possible to prove that the arrangement was a sham, and that you are a tenant in the normal way.

B. Grounds for possession

Assuming the tenancy is now statutory, because the

contractual tenancy has come to an end properly (above, and Chapter 4), and that none of the foregoing remarks mean that you have ceased to be a protected tenant, the only way you can be made to leave is if the landlord can get an order of the court. The only way the landlord can get an order of the court is by proving that there are 'grounds for possession'.

There are two classes of 'ground for possession'. In the first class, the landlord has to show that certain facts exist, *and* that it is *reasonable* to make an order. This class is known as the 'discretionary' grounds, because it is up to the discretion of the judge whether or not it is reasonable to make the order. In the second class, the landlord has only to show that certain facts exist, and there is no overriding requirement to show that it is reasonable; this class is known as the 'mandatory' grounds.

(a) The discretionary grounds. In relation to these 'grounds for possession', the landlord must show *both* that the specified facts exist, *and* that it is reasonable to make an order for possession. It is for the landlord to show that both of these ingredients are present, not for you to prove that they are not.

Reasonableness. The purpose of this overriding requirement of reasonableness is to ensure that you do not lose your home because of some trivial breach of a term of the tenancy, or because the landlord has written some particularly onerous term into the tenancy, or because of some minor misdemeanour in relation to neighbours, or because of some minor damage to the property or furniture that could easily be put right.

An example of a case where it was held not reasonable to make the tenant leave was when an elderly couple who had lived for many years in the property in question fell on hard times. He lost his job; she was ill. They fell into arrears of rent. They had always been good tenants before these misfortunes; it would have been wrong to make them lose their home in these circumstances.

When deciding whether or not it is reasonable to make an order for possession, the court will take all the circumstances into account, both those affecting you, and those affecting the landlord. Whether you have been a good tenant, or the landlord a good landlord, will be relevant; e.g. how long you have been in occupation, and whether the facts which give rise to the ground for possession amount to a serious default or not.

In one case, a tenant was convicted of using premises for the purposes of smoking cannabis; he was punished by the criminal courts. Then the landlord claimed possession, on the ground (see below) known as 'illegal user'. The court decided that to turn the tenant out would be to punish him twice for the same offence. But in that case, there were no other defaults, such as general misconduct, nuisance to neighbours, rent arrears.

It is better not to allow the landlord to 'get to first base', by producing one of the grounds for possession at all, than to have to rely on the court's view of what is reasonable; on the other hand, the fact that the landlord is able to produce a ground for possession (more common than any other is rent arrears) should not frighten you into quitting before the court decides whether or not you have to.

Tenant's default. The first group of grounds for possession, in relation to which the court has to be satisfied that it is reasonable to make you quit, is: rent arrears, breach of term of tenancy, nuisance and annoyance to adjoining occupiers, damage to premises or furniture provided by the landlord, illegal or immoral use of premises. If rent arrears can be cleared before the case actually comes to court, it is unusual for an order to be made unless there has been a history of delay; even if they have not been cleared, unless they have mounted very high indeed, you will normally be given an opportunity to clear them over a period of time, without losing your home.

In most of these cases, if the actual default was caused by your sub-tenant or lodger, the court will not be able to make an order if you have done everything you can to evict the sub-tenant or lodger.

In addition, it is a ground for possession that you have given a valid notice to quit to your landlord and in reliance upon it he or she has arranged to let the premises to someone else or to sell them (see Chapter 4). If you let the landlord know that you have changed your mind and do not intend to go, before he or she acts on the notice, the ground will not apply. It still has to be reasonable to make you leave.

Whether or not your tenancy permits subletting (see Chapter 1) or assignment (see Chapter 6), if you have sublet or assigned the whole of the premises, there will be a ground for possession against you *and* against the sub-tenant or assignee. (Indeed, in any of these cases the same ground that may be used against you may be used against your sub-tenant: but in all of them, the landlord has to show that it is reasonable to evict each of you, i.e. tenant and sub-tenant, and that has to be considered separately for each of you.)

A subletting of the whole of the premises may be in one subletting, or by subletting of different parts at different times, until the whole has been sublet. If the tenancy agreement prohibits subletting or assignment, then unless the breach has been 'waived' (see Chapters 1 and 6) there will be *two* grounds: breach of term of tenancy, and subletting/assignment. A subletting of part only will be a breach of a term of the tenancy if the agreement prohibits any subletting, and the breach has not been waived. A letting to a lodger (i.e. licensee), or sharing, will not give rise to this subletting/assignment ground, nor indeed will it be a breach of a term of the tenancy unless that term *also* covers lodgers and sharers.

A further ground for possession will exist if there is a

rent registered for the premises, or part of them, with the Rent Officer or the Rent Tribunal (see Chapter 8) and you have been charging your sub-tenant more than is permitted. Again, in theory, this ground could be used against both you *and* your sub-tenant, but it is almost inconceivable that it would ever be reasonable to make an order against the sub-tenant for permitting himself or herself to be overcharged.

No-fault grounds. There is a number of further grounds which do not imply any fault on your part. These are still grounds in relation to which the landlord has to show *both* that the relevant conditions are fulfilled *and* that it is reasonable to make an order against you.

There is a ground which is available against a service tenant (see Chapter 1) to whom a letting was given in consequence of the employment and the tenant is the *landlord's* employee. This is quite important: if the landlord is an individual but employs the tenant through a company, this ground will not apply. Nor will it apply if the landlord is just one of a number of partners who together employ the tenant. Nor will it apply if the tenancy preceded the employment, because the letting will not be *in consequence of* the employment.

The ground is only available if you are no longer in your landlord's employment, and the landlord wants the property for some other full-time employee, or some person who has been given a contract for full-time employment which is conditional on the landlord finding him or her somewhere to live.

The second 'no-fault' ground is more common. This arises when the landlord says that he or she wants to live in your premises himself or herself, or wants it for one of a specified list of relatives (children over 18 years old, parents or parents-in-law). This has to be a reasonable requirement on the part of the landlord, and it must be the landlord's intention that he or she or one of the relatives will actually live in the premises, as a home, for a while, not merely, for example, for a short time until the property can be sold.

A company landlord cannot use this ground, because it cannot and does not 'live'. A landlord who says that he or she is quitting some mansion in a smart part of town may have a hard time convincing a court that it is really the intention to live in a small flat or house in a cheap part of town, unless, of course, he or she is genuinely in financial difficulty.

The ground is not available at all to a landlord who *bought* the premises with you already in occupation, but is available if he or she became the landlord in some other way, for example, because he or she inherited it.

In relation to this ground, you will have a special and additional defence. Even if the landlord does reasonably want the premises for his or her, or a relative's, occupation, no order will be made if it would cause greater hardship for you to leave than to make the landlord find somewhere else. While the landlord has to prove that a ground for possession exists, and that it is reasonable to make the order, *you* have to show greater hardship.

In addition to the possibility that the landlord is better off than you, either in cash terms or because he or she can mortgage the property, other factors may be relevant: nearness of relatives, work, other facilities (for instance, a church).

In either of these two cases – wanted for employee, or for landlord or landlord's relative – a tenant who is ordered to leave may claim compensation through the courts, if the landlord obtains the order by misrepresentation, by telling an untruth as to (for example) intentions or needs.

There is a third 'no-fault' discretionary ground for possession and this, too, is common. This is that, as and when you have to go, there will be suitable alternative accommodation available for you. The landlord need not provide the alternative accommodation; it could be available from the local authority, or it could even be that you have somewhere else of your own. Indeed, if you have a tenancy that is too large for your needs, the landlord can try to reclaim some of the property by offering you a new tenancy of part only of your existing accommodation (i.e. the part you actually live in).

If somewhere else is offered, it has to be 'suitable' in the sense that it is big enough for you and your family (but not merely a friend who happens to live with you, although this may affect whether or not it is reasonable to make an order), near enough to your work, and subject to as much security of tenure (it would not be suitable if, for example, it would be a shorthold tenancy, or subject to a mandatory ground – see page 115). If you are offered an *assured* tenancy (see Chapter 3), the court may, or may not, consider that this affords suitable security, but it will not do so if the assured is an assured shorthold, or if it is subject to an assured, mandatory ground notice. You should ask the court to order that your new tenancy be protected instead of assured.

The premises must also be similar to your present accommodation, or otherwise suitable, as regards 'character'. This brings in questions of environment: a letting of a flat above a chip shop is no substitute for a house in a quiet, residential street. Finally, the alternative accommodation must be suitable as regards rent, but, with the availability of housing benefit, this tends to play a less important part in the decision because a court will assume that if you cannot afford the new rent there will be assistance available.

Not uncommonly, during the course of a hearing a landlord will make 'offers', such as to pay removal expenses, reinstall telephone or services, do decorations or even improvements or conversions. When fighting a case, it is tempting to say: 'I won't move, whatever is done.' It is worthwhile paying attention to these 'offers', because you may have to move at the end of the day, and if such offers are taken seriously enough by the court, they are unlikely to be valueless. If such offers are made, the court should always be asked to record them. An order can be made conditional on compliance with an offer, or postponed until an offer is fulfilled.

Types of order. In *all* of these cases, the reasonableness requirement is the fall-back. A minor nuisance or annoy- ance, or one of temporary duration, a small offence, petty damage to premises or furniture which can easily be put right, short-lived rent arrears and so on, ought not to lead to outright eviction.

In the same way, the landlord may have a very strong case of needing premises for an employee, or for himself or herself or family, and yet, when everything is taken into account, it is simply not reasonable to make you go. This is particularly so on the question of suitable alter- native accommodation: everything may be 'just right' with the new accommodation, but some other factor says that you shouldn't have to go; for example, how long you have lived in an area, how close the ties, the fact that you have a friend living with you although they are not a member of your family, and if compelled to move you will not be able to go on living together.

One way in which the courts can resolve the difficult balance between grounds for possession, reasonableness, and extent of default or other circumstances, is by the different types of orders which they may make. These are only available in the case of these discretionary grounds. All orders will be made conditional on payment of any arrears of rent there may be, and on payment of current rent, unless the court is of the view that it would cause exceptional hardship to impose such conditions, or would otherwise be unreasonable.

If the court has decided that you have to go, it can make an outright order for possession. This will normally mean that you have to leave in four to six weeks' time. However, a longer period – perhaps much longer – can be given, for instance because of a greater hardship issue, or because you are to be made to move somewhere else, after many years in one place. Similarly, an order might be deferred pending works to suitable alternative accommodation.

Another formulation is the 'suspended order'. This is an order under which the court says that you can stay, provided some incident does not recur, or you comply with a condition, such as payment of arrears at so-and-so much per week, no further rent arrears, no more nuisance, or remedying damage to premises or furniture.

Whatever class of order is made, at any time before it is actually carried out (which means the date stated by the court rather than the period between that date and the date of actual eviction by bailiff), you can apply to the court to vary the order, to give further time, to remove a condition, or even to turn an outright order into a conditional or suspended order. For example, you may have been unable to clear arrears, but suddenly find that money is available after all; or else, having agreed to pay £5 per week off arrears, you lose your job and cannot afford to maintain the payment; or you become ill.

If any such circumstance seems relevant, and likely to persuade the court to alter an order, you should always apply to the court for variation, rather than wait for the order to be carried out and then bring up the new argument. You should also apply to a court to discharge an order which was conditional, once the condition has been fulfilled. For example, you are allowed to stay on payment of the arrears. Once the arrears have been cleared, ask for the court to discharge the order entirely, rather than leave it on file, because otherwise if arrears happen again, the landlord may be able to use the old order, instead of having to get a new one.

(b) Mandatory grounds. The second group of grounds for possession is called the mandatory grounds, because there is no overriding requirement of 'reasonableness'. The landlord need only show that the relevant or specified preconditions exist. Furthermore, there is little discretion as to the sort of order that can be made. If the landlord is successful in proving that the ground exists, the court must make an order for possession, to take effect in no more than two weeks, unless exceptional hardship would be caused, in which case the order can be extended, but only to a maximum of six weeks.

There are ten 'mandatory' grounds, but one of these is applicable to protected shorthold tenancies only, and is accordingly considered separately below. No attention need be paid to four grounds which relate to property which has been occupied at some time in the past, before the present tenant was let into occupation, by ministers of religion, or people employed in agriculture. These are grounds which are rarely used nowadays. They all require some degree of prior warning by way of written notice to the tenant that they may be applicable, so that the tenant has ample opportunity to take advice as to what his or her exact position is.

Two of the remaining five grounds can also be described fairly easily. One of these applies to 'out-of-season lettings' or, as they are sometimes called, 'winter lets'. The intention is that people who customarily let out accommodation for holiday purposes, i.e. on holiday lettings (see Chapter 3), should be able to let them out on normal lettings, at times of the year when there are no visitors.

A protected tenancy will only be subject to this mandatory ground for possession if it is a fixed-term tenancy, for not more than eight months. During the year before the letting, the premises must have been let out on a holiday tenancy. Finally, the tenant must have been given written notice at the beginning of the tenancy that this 'ground' would apply.

A similar ground for possession is available in relation to premises normally let out to students (see Chapter 3). Again, written notice must be given at the start of the tenancy, the tenancy must be a fixed-term tenancy, although in this case for up to one year, and during the year preceding the start of the letting the premises must have been let out on a student tenancy.

The remaining three mandatory grounds have much in common. The first of these grounds is for the temporarily absent 'owner occupier'. The second is for retirement homes. The third is for servicemen and servicewomen.

In the first case, the property must formerly have been occupied by the landlord as a residence; since the landlord last occupied the premises as a residence, the premises must not have been let out to anyone without the landlord giving that person a notice in writing to the effect that this mandatory ground might apply against them; and, no later than at the beginning of your tenancy, the landlord must have given you a notice to the same effect.

In the second case, the property must be property which the landlord intends to occupy on retirement from regular employment; since 14 August 1974 (the date the Rent Act 1974 was introduced, bringing this ground with it – see also Chapter 3), the premises must not have been let out to anyone without the landlord giving that person a notice in writing to the effect that this mandatory ground might apply against them; and, no later than at the beginning of your tenancy, the landlord must have given you a notice to the same effect.

In the third case, the property must be owned by someone who was, at the time he or she bought the property *and* at the commencement of your tenancy, a member of the armed forces; since 28 November 1980 (the date this provision was introduced), the premises must not have been let out to anyone without the landlord giving that person a notice in writing to the effect that this mandatory ground might apply against them; and, no later than at the beginning of your tenancy, the landlord must have given you a notice to the same effect.

In any of these cases, if the landlord omitted to give you a notice at the beginning of your tenancy, or else if it can be shown that on a previous letting the landlord omitted to give a former tenant the notice that the ground might apply, the court can waive the requirement if it thinks it is just and equitable to do so: for example if the failure was a technical failure because it was oral rather than in writing, or if it was a day or so late and you were offered the chance of leaving and had not actually prejudiced your own position (for example, by quitting somewhere else), and in any case if there is no real prejudice to you (such as that because you thought you were protected indefinitely, you have spent a great deal of money on the premises, or put down other roots of similar importance).

The mere fact that all of these conditions are fulfilled is still not enough to ensure that the landlord can recover possession. The landlord must also demonstrate that one or more of a series of what might be called 'current conditions' are fulfilled.

There are seven current conditions, one or more of which must be demonstrated. They do not all apply to each of these three grounds. In the first case, the landlord must be able to show numbers 2 or numbers 4–7; in the second case, the landlord must be able to show one of the numbers 3–7; in the third case, the landlord must be able to show number 1, or numbers 4–7.

The current conditions are:
1. Owner wants the premises to live in.
2. Either the owner, or someone who lived with him or

her when the owner last used the premises as a home, wants the premises to live in.

3. The owner has retired from regular employment, and wants to live in the premises.

4. The owner has died, and the dwelling is required as a residence for a member of the owner's family who was living with him or her at the time of death.

5. The owner has died, and the dwelling is required by whoever has inherited the property, either to live in, or to sell with vacant possession.

6. The property is subject to a mortgage, which was created before the tenancy was granted and the mortgage company wants the property empty in order to sell it (i.e. because the landlord has defaulted on the mortgage payments).

7. The owner finds that the property is no longer suitable to his or her needs, having regard to his or her place of employment (for example, because he or she has come back from abroad after letting the premises out for a while, and his or her workplace has been moved), and the owner wants the property empty in order to sell it and buy somewhere more suitable for himself or herself.

What security does a protected shorthold tenant have?

Protected shorthold tenancy is modelled on protected tenancy. The initial tenancy will have been for from one to five years, and only you can 'break' it within that period, unless the landlord can forfeit for breach of a term of the tenancy (see Chapter 3). Once the initial fixed-term tenancy comes to an end, if the landlord does not, or cannot, start the eviction procedures described below, you will be able to stay on, either automatically as a periodic (but still protected shorthold) tenant, or under a new fixed-term agreement between you and the landlord.

There are two sorts of way in which a protected

shorthold tenant can be evicted. First of all, if you breach a term of your tenancy, and the landlord forfeits, or if after the initial fixed term you have a periodic tenancy and the landlord brings that to an end by notice to quit, you can be evicted in exactly the same way as if you were an ordinary, protected tenant, i.e. the landlord can use any of the grounds for possession described above, in relation to protected tenants (for example, rent arrears, plus reasonableness). In effect, the fact that you are a protected shorthold tenant may be ignored.

The second way is by use of the protected shorthold procedure. This operates as a mandatory ground for possession (see page 115). That means that once it is successfully activated by the landlord, the court has no greater discretion than to give you up to two weeks, or six weeks in a case of exceptional hardship.

At the same time as, or before, your tenancy was granted, your landlord ought to have given you a protected shorthold notice, in the prescribed form (see Chapter 3). However, as with some of the other mandatory grounds, if the landlord failed to do this, the court can waive the requirement, on the basis that it is 'just and equitable' to do so. This the court should not do, unless it is quite clear that you were well aware all along that your tenancy was meant to be a protected shorthold tenancy, and that only some technical or minor failure on the part of the landlord led to the omission to issue the right kind of notice (such as because the form of notice had changed, and the landlord issued an old one instead of a new one).

To operate the protected shorthold ground, once eviction is intended, the landlord must also serve you with a 'warning notice' that it is intended to seek to repossess the premises. It will be recalled that protected shorthold tenancies are, at least initially, fixed term. A warning notice can only be served within the three months before the fixed term is due to expire, or during the same three months in any following year. This is the 'shorthold season'.

This notice must be in writing. It must give a minimum of three months' warning, but there is no maximum period. On the face of it, this would suggest that you could be kept permanently under a shorthold warning notice, i.e. by serving an annual notice to last one year. The law prohibits this. It does this in two ways. First of all, proceedings for possession have to be started after the period of warning notice has expired, but within three months of the expiry. Secondly, there must be a gap of three months between the expiry of the shorthold warning notice and the service of a new notice.

An example may help. A fixed term is granted on 1 April 1984, to expire on 31 March 1986. A warning notice may be served at any time between the beginning of January and the end of March during 1986, or any subsequent year so long as you stay on as a protected shorthold tenant. It must give you at least three months' warning: if served on 1 January, therefore, proceedings could commence on 1 April; if not served until 1 March, however, they could not commence before 1 June. If the landlord gave longer than three months, the proceedings could not commence until the time allowed had expired.

Once the notice expires, the landlord must bring the proceedings within three months, or else the notice lapses and the landlord will have to start again. He or she cannot serve a further notice during the next three months. Thus, if the notice was for three months, and was served on 1 January, proceedings must be commenced between 1 April and 30 June, and during that time no further notice can be served. Accordingly, 1 July would be the earliest date when a new notice could be served, but as the notice can only be served during the shorthold season (January–

March), the landlord cannot serve a further notice until 1 January next.

If, however, the landlord gives nine months, from 1 January, he or she can commence proceedings at any time between 1 October and 30 December; if he or she fails to do so, he or she can serve a new notice immediately after 30 December, as (a) the landlord will be back in the shorthold season, and (b) three months will have passed since the last notice lapsed.

What security does an assured tenant have?

If you are an assured tenant, you can continue to live in your premises for the rest of your life, *provided* you remain an assured tenant, and *unless* the landlord gets an order for your eviction (and therefore for the termination of your tenancy: see Chapter 4). A spouse may be able to take over the tenancy on your death (see Chapter 6).

A. *Is tenancy still assured?*

There is a small number of circumstances in which a tenancy which has been assured may not be so by the time the landlord seeks to evict you. If the tenancy has ceased to be assured, then you will have become an unprotected tenant, and your only protection will be the requirement that the landlord brings the contractual tenancy to an end in the normal way applicable to unprotected tenants (see Chapter 4), *rather than* by the procedure of notice of seeking possession applicable to assured tenants (see Chapter 4). The point is, you will not be an assured tenant any more.

There are considerable similarities with protected tenants, and accordingly some of the provisions can be described by cross-reference.

(a) Change of landlord. The remarks made under this heading, in relation to protected tenants, apply in exactly

the same way to assured tenants (see page 103).

(b) Public Health. The position is the same as in relation to protected tenants (see page 103), *save* that illegal overcrowding does not cause you to cease to be an assured tenant. Again, where these provisions apply to take away your protection as an assured tenant, you will almost certainly be rehoused by the local authority.

(c) Use of premises. The remarks made under this heading, in relation to protected tenants (see page 103) apply in exactly the same way to assured tenants.

(d) Non-use of premises. This is the most important and most common reason why a tenancy which is or has been assured ceases to be so: it is a continuing requirement that the tenant (or if a joint tenancy, at least one of the tenants) uses the premises as an only or principal home (see page 105). This is not the same test as the 'residence' test described on page 104 in relation to protected tenants whose tenancies have become statutory, and who can sustain protection if they are using the premises as 'a' residence (even if they have another); the test for *assured* tenants is that the premises are being used as an *only* home, or a *principal* home, and this residential requirement has to be maintained at all times.

Of course, you do not have to sleep in the premises every night: you are entitled to holidays, or a second home (so long as that second home is in the nature of an occasional or holiday home). If you go into hospital, then your home remains such, at least until it is known that you can never return. If you go to look after a relative for a period of time, you are likely still to be considered to be using your home as an only or principal home. But if you go away for a long period of time – voluntarily or not – it may become difficult to claim that the property is your home (even if you have no other), and if you sublet the whole of the premises (see Chapter 1), it will be impossible to maintain that it is still your home.

Because the law is relatively new, it is difficult indeed to predict or describe how the courts will apply the phrase 'only or principal home'. It will be clear in the majority of cases, and in those cases where there is doubt you should take advice (see Chapter 10), particularly if you can do so before you change your place of residence, temporarily or permanently.

The remarks made above in relation to protected tenants, and 'company lettings' designed to show that – in this case – the letting is not to an individual (see page 106), as well as that the individual is not in residence, apply similarly to assured tenancies.

B. *Grounds for possession.*

Like protected tenants (see page 106), the grounds for possession against assured tenants are divided into two classes: (a) where the landlord has to show *both* that certain facts exist *and* that it is reasonable to make an order of the court (discretionary grounds); and (b) those where he or she needs only show that the facts exist (mandatory grounds). What is meant by 'reasonable' is exactly the same as described in relation to protected tenants; the same types of order described above in relation to protected tenants are available in the same circumstances: a suspended or outright order in the case of possession on a discretionary ground; an outright order only in the case of a mandatory ground.

It is the grounds themselves, and whether or not they are discretionary, which are different, although some of them are the same. In *all* cases, however, if the landlord secures an order for possession against you by misrepresenting the facts to the court, or concealing them, you are entitled to go back to the court to seek a compensation order from the landlord. Remember, however, that misrepresentation or concealment are not the same as a genuine change of mind, e.g. whether a landlord intends to live in premises (see further below, under the mandatory grounds).

(a) Discretionary grounds. Tenant's default. Some of the grounds described in relation to protected tenants under this heading (see page 108) apply also to assured tenants: breach of term of tenancy; nuisance and annoyance to adjoining occupiers (if by sub-tenant or lodger, without your having done all you can to evict him or her); damage to premises or furniture; illegal or immoral use of premises.

But there is no ground concerning services by you of notice to quit, for if you have served notice to quit *you* will have terminated your assured tenancy, and lost it: there is no 'statutory tenancy' which follows (see Chapter 4). There is also no ground concerning assignment or subletting of the whole of your premises, because you will have ceased to qualify as an *assured* tenant, for want of residence. There is no ground concerning overcharging a sub-tenant.

The position is also different so far as it concerns arrears of rent. In the case of protected tenants, there was one, general, discretionary ground concerning arrears.

In the case of assured tenants, there are no less than three. One of these is *mandatory* (one quarter's arrears: see further below). Two of them are discretionary: that there were rent arrears both at the date of the notice of seeking possession and at the date proceedings are begun; and, whether or not there were arrears when the proceedings were begun, that you have persistently delayed paying rent lawfully due. Because of the way these grounds are worded, it cannot be said, in the case of an assured tenant, that an order will not usually be made if arrears are cleared before the hearing.

However, the first of these two discretionary arrears grounds requires arrears *both* when the notice of seeking possession is served, *and* when the proceedings are commenced, so that if arrears are paid off before the proceedings are begun (which will normally mean a minimum of four weeks after the notice of seeking possession is served: see Chapter 4), the ground will not be available against you. Only if the landlord has to repeat this process, because you persistently delay paying rent until notice of seeking possession is served, will the second of these two discretionary arrears grounds be available against you.

No-fault grounds. In the case of an assured tenant who is a former employee of the landlord, the position is similar, but not identical, to that of a protected tenant (see page 110). There is a discretionary ground (i.e. one where the landlord must still show that it is reasonable to make the order) that you were let the premises in consequence of your employment, by either the current or a previous landlord, and that your employment has ceased.

The second of the grounds which appeared in relation to protected tenants under this heading does not apply to assured tenants, though a similar ground is available to a landlord as a *mandatory* ground (see further below). But the third ground which appeared in relation to protected tenants under this heading applies also to assured tenants: that is, that suitable alternative accommodation will be available for you (and that it is reasonable to make you move). The remarks concerning protected tenants (see page 111) apply in the same way to assured tenants (save that you cannot, of course, ask the court to make you a protected tenant). Note, however, that if an assured tenant has to move on this ground, you have a right to your reasonable removal expenses, payable by the landlord.

(b) Mandatory grounds. These are the grounds where the landlord need only show that the facts apply, not additionally that it is reasonable to make the order. Most of the mandatory grounds applicable to assured tenants are sufficiently dissimilar to those applicable to protected

tenants to require their own description. There are eight of them. Two of them are identical to those applicable to protected tenants and can be described by cross-reference (see page 115): normally let to students; and, out-of-season 'winter-lets' of holiday accommodation. In addition, possession can be claimed of property held to be available for a minister of religion, which is now required for the use of such. In all of these cases, the landlord must have given written notice no later than the beginning of the tenancy that possession might be recovered on these grounds, and there is no discretion on the part of a court to 'waive' this requirement.

A court *can*, however, waive the requirement for prior notice, *if*, but only if, it considers it just and equitable to do so (see page 117 in relation to protected tenants), in the case of landlords who fall within one of the following classes:

1. Prior to the grant of the tenancy, the landlord (or if joint landlords, at least one of them) used to live in the premises, as an only or principal home (whether or not he or she owned the premises at that time).

2. The landlord (or if joint landlords, at least one of them) now wants the premises as his or her only or principal home, or an only or principal home for a spouse. In this case, however, the ground is not available if the landlord (or if joint landlords, any one of them) became a landlord by buying the property with you already in it, whether the purchase was for money, or some other valuable consideration.

In these cases, then, there is a ground for possession available against you, but the landlord will have to have given notice in writing no later than the beginning of the tenancy that it might be used, unless the court decides that it is just and equitable to let the landlord use the ground without having given such notice.

3. A further mandatory ground, which similarly

requires prior written notice unless the court decides to waive the requirement on the basis that it is just and equitable to do so, is that the property is subject to a mortgage, which preceded your tenancy, and the mortgage company now wishes to sell the property, with vacant possession, i.e. in order to recover the money it has advanced to your landlord.

4. Another new and mandatory ground is available to your landlord if he or she wishes to demolish the property, or reconstruct the whole of it or a substantial part of it, or otherwise carry out substantial works on the whole or a substantial part of it or on a building of which it forms part, e.g. a block of flats.

This ground is only available, however, if the landlord *either* owned the premises before your tenancy began (or a previous assured tenancy) either as a sole or a joint tenant, *or* became landlord without actually having to pay anything for the property, e.g. a transfer between related companies, where a different company owned the property when you moved in, but transferred ownership to another company who has become your landlord and now is to carry out the works.

This ground is also only available if the works cannot reasonably be carried out without you giving up possession, either temporarily while the work is being carried out, or permanently because the whole or part of your dwelling is to be demolished.

Provided the property will substantially exist after the works, or a similar property is available, sufficient for you and your family to live in, the landlord will not be able to use this ground if you agree to the change – temporary or permanent. If you do agree, you should ensure that any agreement is in writing, e.g. how long the works will take, where you will stay during the works, who will pay, that you have a right to return, and so on. If you have to move out permanently on this ground, you have a right to your reasonable removal expenses, payable by the landlord.

The ground is not available if the tenant became an assured tenant by reason of succession under the Rent Act (see Chapter 6: normally, a successor under the Rent Act becomes a protected tenant; in some circumstances, however, he or she becomes an assured tenant instead).

5. The next new and mandatory ground for possession arises on the death of an assured tenant. We will see in Chapter 6 that a tenancy can pass under a will, or on intestacy; it can also pass by a process known as 'statutory succession', i.e. where Parliament has dictated who may inherit. This ground applies *only* where the inheritance is under a will or on intestacy, and does not apply where provision is made for statutory succession.

On the face of it, if you thus inherit someone else's assured tenancy, you become the assured tenant yourself. However, if the landlord brings possession proceedings against you within 12 months of the death of the previous tenant – or within 12 months of when a court decides that the landlord (or if joint landlords, one of them) learned of the death of the previous tenant – you can be evicted.

6. Finally, there is the *mandatory* ground which applies in the case of rent arrears, as distinct from the two discretionary grounds described above. You can be evicted if both at the date of the notice of seeking possession, and at the date of the actual hearing in a court of the claim for possession, you were at least one quarter's rent in arrears (thirteen weeks or three months). The dangers, therefore, of allowing yourself to fall into such a sum of arrears, are considerable.

What security does an assured shorthold tenant have?

An assured shorthold tenant can be evicted on any of the grounds described above; in addition, he or she can be evicted simply by reason of the special notice of seeking possession described in relation to assured shorthold tenants in Chapter 4.

What security goes with a restricted contract?

Occupiers who have restricted contracts (Chapter 3) have the security afforded them under their contracts, be they tenancies or licences, until the tenancy or licence is brought to an end properly (see Chapter 4).

The security provisions governing restricted contracts, whether they are tenancies or licences, are different, depending on whether the contract started before 28 November 1980 (the date when relevant provisions of the Housing Act 1980 came into force) or on or after that date (but of course, before 15 January 1989, when the Housing Act 1988 came into force and prevented the creation of any new restricted contracts: see Chapter 3).

A. Contracts after 1980 Act

If a restricted contract started on or after 28 November 1980, the security provisions are extremely simple to describe. They are the same whether the contract was periodic, or fixed term, and whether a tenancy or a licence. The landlord must always go to court to get an order, and the court has power to grant up to a total of three months' additional time, from the date of the court hearing, and whether three months is granted in one go, or whether time is granted in smaller periods. Thus, if the court initially grants only one month, you can apply for an extension, but you cannot do so if the court initially grants the full three months.

If the court is willing to grant a period of time, it will always be on conditions to pay off any arrears of rent that there may be, and to maintain current payments, unless the court is satisfied that it would cause exceptional hardship to do this, or that it would otherwise be unreasonable.

B. Contracts from before 1980 Act

The position governing restricted contracts which date from before 28 November 1980 is more complicated. A distinction must be drawn between periodic contracts, and those for a fixed term.

(a) Fixed-term contracts. In relation to fixed-term contracts, whether tenancy or licence, the position can be stated simply: there is no security available beyond the contract itself, whether from court or from anywhere else. The landlord must, however, still seek a court order against a former fixed-term *tenant,* but the court will allow the tenant no more than two weeks in which to go, unless this would cause exceptional hardship in which case the maximum time is six weeks.

(b) Periodic contracts. The security available to periodic tenants, and to periodic licensees, whose contracts started before 28 November 1980, is the power to refer a notice to quit, or a notice to terminate a licence, to the Rent Tribunal. Provided the notice is referred to the Rent Tribunal before it expires (see Chapter 4), the Rent Tribunal may defer the notice for up to six months *at a time.*

In theory, a Rent Tribunal can go on deferring a notice for as long as it wishes, although in practice it is extremely uncommon for more than one period of six months to be allowed, or for more than six or nine months in all to be allowed. So long as the notice stands deferred, the contract (tenancy or licence) has in law not come to an end, and therefore the landlord cannot make the occupier leave.

In addition, in Chapter 8 I shall describe your (still existing) right to refer a rent to the Rent Tribunal. In relation to these pre-1980 Act contracts, if you refer the rent to the Rent Tribunal, and the landlord retaliates with a notice to quit or notice to terminate the licence, then without any application to the Tribunal at all, the notice is automatically deferred for six months, *unless* either you withdraw the rent reference, or when the Tribunal hears the rent reference it decides that the 'automatic' deferral should be for a shorter period.

Whether security is obtained by application for security after receipt of a notice, or automatically in the case of a retaliatory notice following a rent reference, during the period of referral the landlord can apply back to the Tribunal for the period to be reduced because you are in breach of a term of the contract (for instance, rent arrears), or have been a nuisance or annoyance to adjoining occupiers, or have used the premises for an illegal or immoral purpose, or have allowed the premises or furniture to deteriorate.

In addition, the *court* has the same power as the Tribunal to reduce this security (even though it was initially granted either by the Tribunal, or automatically), and this it may do on exactly the same grounds. If a reduction order is made, whether by Tribunal or court, you cannot reapply to the Tribunal for a further period of security.

6: Who Can Live in the Premises?

Can I let whomever I like live in the premises?
Normally, yes. A few agreements will state that *only* you
can occupy premises, and if you let someone else live with
you, you will be in breach of that term. If you have a
protected or assured tenancy (see Chapter 3) and the
landlord seeks possession on the ground of this breach
(see Chapter 5), it is not very likely that you will be
evicted, unless there are good reasons for limiting the
occupation of the premises (for example, strain on shared
facilities, or a constant stream of sharers causing disturbance, etc).

A 'no children' requirement of a tenancy may well be
considered contrary to public policy, unless there is a resident landlord (in which case you will probably not have
much if any security in any event), or the house was full
of elderly people at the time your tenancy was granted.
The position may be different, however, if you allow the
premises to be occupied by so many people that it
becomes overcrowded in law (see below).

Can I let someone in as my sub-tenant?
This depends on whether the tenancy agreement or the
law prohibits or restricts subletting. The position has been
described in Chapter 1, including the possibility that an
illegal subletting becomes legal by 'waiver'. If you are a
licensee, any occupiers you let in will also be licensees, not
sub-tenants.

Can I let someone in as my licensee or lodger?
Again this depends on what the agreement says. If it only
forbids or restricts subletting, you have not broken a term

of the agreement by taking in a lodger or licensee. Otherwise, the position is as described in answer to the first question of this chapter (see above).

How many people can I allow to live in the premises?

Subject to the terms of the agreement (last question), you may let however many people you like live in the premises, *provided* it does not become overcrowded in law (see below).

What is overcrowding in law?

Premises are overcrowded when specified standards are offended. The standards apply to the 'home': a house, or a flat or a room – whatever it is that you have rented. The home will be overcrowded whenever there are so many people living in it that any two or more people of the opposite sex (of 10 years of age or more) and who are not living together as husband and wife (whether or not legally married) have to sleep in the same room.

This does not mean as much as it at first sounds, because it is not only bedrooms which are taken into account, but any 'living-rooms', meaning *not only* a bedroom, and a living-room itself, *but also* a kitchen big enough to accommodate a bed. It follows that the test is not whether two or more people at least 10 years old and of the opposite sex (other than husband and wife) *are* sleeping in the same room, but whether, by counting 'heads' and 'rooms', they *have* to do so.

However, there is a maximum of two persons to any one living-room, and this only applies if a room measures at least 110 square feet. In smaller rooms the maximum numbers are: less than 50 square feet, no one to occupy; 50 to less than 70 square feet, half a person; 70 to less than 90 square feet, one person; 90 to less than 110 square feet, one and a half people.

Furthermore, where there are only two rooms in the

home, there is a maximum of three people who may live in it; three rooms, five persons; four rooms, seven and a half persons; five rooms or more, ten persons plus two people for each room more than five (that means in six rooms, twelve people; seven rooms, fourteen people, and so on). The references to 'half' a person are not a joke: children up to the age of one year do not count at all; those aged from one to (and including) nine years count as a half.

To work out if there is overcrowding, then, start with the simpler calculation: allocate the right number of people to the right number of rooms. If this suggests the premises are *not* overcrowded, check room sizes to see if as many people are allowed to occupy each of the rooms under the second calculation.

Thus, there may be five people living in a house with three living-rooms, but when one of the rooms is measured it is found to be less than 70 square feet, in which case either a half, or no person can occupy it, so that the maximum would be four, or four and a half.

There are, however, two circumstances when what appears to be overcrowding is *not* treated as such in law. First, permission may be sought and obtained from the local authority, for 'licensed' overcrowding for a period of up to one year at a time. Only you (not a landlord) can apply for such permission, and the permission must state the number who are allowed to stay. Secondly, purely temporary overcrowding, caused by a visit from a member of your family, is disregarded.

Can I find out if my premises are overcrowded other than by working it out for myself?

Yes. Rent books (see Chapter 2) have to contain a summary of these overcrowding provisions, a note about the possibility of getting permission for overcrowding from the local authority, *and*, most important of all, a statement of how many occupiers are permitted. Either you or the landlord can ask the local authority to provide a written statement as to how many people are capable of living in a property without causing it to be overcrowded. This may be done at the beginning of occupation, or at any time.

What happens if premises are overcrowded?

If you allow premises to become overcrowded in law, you will commit an offence; if you are a protected tenant, you will also lose your protection (see Chapter 5). (The same applies to a protected shorthold tenant, but *not* to an assured or an assured shorthold tenant.) No offence is committed (and therefore protection is not lost), however, if the overcrowding has resulted from 'natural growth'. Natural growth occurs when a child of the family reaches a relevant age (i.e. one or 10 years old).

To secure the protection of the 'natural growth' defence, though, either before the child reaches the relevant age or before any prosecution is instituted for illegal overcrowding, you have to have applied to the local authority for rehousing, and not refused an offer from them. Nor will the defence apply if you have the opportunity to reduce the overcrowding by asking a lodger, who is not a member of your family, to leave, and the occupier fails to do so. You only have to ask a lodger to leave if it is reasonably practical for the lodger to go, in all the circumstances, having particular regard to whether or not the lodger has anywhere else to move to.

An offer from the authority will only amount to suitable accommodation if you will be able to live in it without overcrowding, *and* the authority certifies that the accommodation is suitable to your needs, as regards security of tenure, proximity to work, financial means, and in other respects. If the authority is offering its own accommodation, it must offer a property with at least two bedrooms (*not* 'any' living room), for four people, three bedrooms for five, and four bedrooms for seven. These are higher standards than the overcrowding standards themselves.

If there is overcrowding, and the natural growth exemption does not apply, however, you will be committing an offence. The local authority is entitled to serve a written notice requesting information about occupation, and it is a further offence to fail to answer or to tell what is known to be an untruth in the answer. In addition, as you will cease to be a protected tenant, if you have been one hitherto, the landlord can take possession proceedings as if you were wholly unprotected. Alternatively, the authority has power to bring proceedings for possession. The authority may also serve a notice on the landlord, informing the landlord of the overcrowding, and if the landlord then fails to bring proceedings, he or she, too, may be considered to have committed an offence.

If I go away for a while, can I transfer my tenancy or licence to someone else during my absence?

If you want to go away for a while, you are likely to want to let someone stay in the property during your absence, both to look after it and probably also to pay the rent and other outgoings. This is not a transfer of the tenancy or licence, which is considered below.

Instead, it is merely a question of letting in someone else as licensee or as a sub-tenant – see Chapter 1 as to the distinction, and see the beginning of this chapter as to whether or not this is permissible. Generally, you will be able to let someone stay in the premises as a licensee, because you will not be creating overcrowding, and it is far more likely that the arrangement between you will be licence not sub-tenancy and, as such, less likely to be prohibited by the agreement.

If you are a protected tenant, whose contract of

tenancy has ended (see Chapter 4), so that you are a statutory tenant, you should bear in mind the need to be able to show that you intend to come back (see Chapter 5). If you are an assured tenant, you must at all times be able to show that, even though someone else is temporarily living in the premises, the premises remain your only or principal home (and bear in mind that only in a small number of cases are you allowed to *sublet,* so that the arrangement ought to be one of licence).

Can I transfer my tenancy or licence to someone else permanently?

None of the provisions we are about to consider will apply when what is involved is transfer of tenancy or licence in the course of a matrimonial breakdown: see *The Divorce Handbook* in this series.

Licences cannot be transferred to someone else, because they are personal rights of occupation. A landlord can, however, always agree to one person taking over from another, in which case the new person will in practice be entering into a new agreement with the landlord.

A protected shorthold tenancy (see Chapter 3) cannot be assigned. A statutory tenancy (which is a protected tenancy – see Chapter 3 – after the contract has been brought properly to an end – see Chapters 4 and 5) cannot be assigned, but it can be transferred, although only by an agreement in writing, to which agreement the landlord is a party – in other words, with the landlord's active consent and participation. Landlords rarely agree to this. The incoming tenant must also sign the written agreement.

It is illegal for the landlord to charge you or the proposed new tenant for his or her agreement, or for you to charge the proposed new tenant for passing on the tenancy (other than a reasonable amount for furniture, fixtures, or for outgoings which refer to the time after you are intended to leave: see Chapter 7).

In other cases, the position is identical to whether you have a right to sublet (see Chapter 1). Thus, the starting-point is whether or not your agreement says anything about assignment. It may prohibit assignment absolutely; this is an absolute prohibition. It may prohibit assignment without the consent of the landlord; this is a qualified prohibition, and consent cannot be unreasonably withheld (Landlord and Tenant Act 1927).

It may say nothing at all about assignment, in which case you are entitled to assign, even without consent, *save* in the case of a periodic or assured shorthold tenancy, in which case the law (Housing Act 1988) implies a qualified covenant that you cannot assign without the consent of the landlord, but the landlord is entitled to withhold consent even unreasonably (although not on grounds which amount to illegal race or sex discrimination; see Chapter 2). This special implied term will, however, only be implied in the same circumstances as for subletting (see page 22), i.e. if the agreement is silent, and you did not pay a premium for it.

All of the observations made in Chapter 1 about the need to seek consent, the landlord's duty to reply in writing to a request in writing, within a reasonable time and giving reasons for a refusal (Landlord and Tenant Act 1988), what may or may not constitute a reasonable refusal, and what to do if the landlord refuses consent, apply to assignment in the same way that they applied to subletting.

To carry out an assignment, it is necessary that it should be by deed – a signed and sealed document, preferably drawn up by a lawyer. If the assignment is not by deed, but the new tenant just moves in, perhaps doing work to the premises, and taking over the rent, he or she will have a valid assignment *as against you.* This is to say you will not be able to revoke the assignment, but it will not become a valid assignment as against the landlord unless it is shown that the landlord has accepted him or her as tenant, for example by accepting rent knowing that it is on the new tenant's own behalf and not just on yours, or by allowing the new tenant to believe he or she has been accepted (and so 'invest' in the tenancy, either financially, such as by redecoration, or in other ways – setting down roots, giving up somewhere else, etc.).

The assignment will, like subletting, either be legal or illegal: it is legal if the agreement does not prohibit or restrict assignment, or if assignment is possible with consent and consent is granted, or if consent cannot be withheld unreasonably and the landlord does, in fact, withhold it unreasonably. In all other cases assignment will be illegal and there will, of course, be a breach of a term of the tenancy. This will affect the new tenant's position, even if the assignment has been carried out validly, i.e. by deed. If the tenancy is fixed term, the fact that there has been a breach by illegal assignment will entitle the landlord to bring the tenancy to an end or seeking possession (see Chapter 4). If periodic, the landlord can in any event always terminate easily by giving notice to quit.

If it is a protected tenancy (see Chapter 3) and the assignment illegal then, although the landlord will still (in the case of periodic or fixed-term tenancies) have to seek a court order, there will be a ground for possession based on the breach of the tenancy agreement, albeit one in relation to which the landlord will also have to show that it is reasonable to make an order (see Chapter 5). In addition, there will be a ground for possession (again, if reasonable) based on the fact that you have assigned the premises (see Chapter 5). This *second* ground will apply, however, *even if the assignment is quite legal.* In each case, though, the key question will be that of whether it is reasonable to make the order, against the assignee (new tenant).

Can my family take over my tenancy or licence?

A transfer between members of the family is an assignment like any other (see last answer). We are concerned here with inheritance. A licence cannot be inherited; a tenancy passes on normally to the next-of-kin, unless you have made a will and specified that someone else is to take over from you as a tenant. The inheritor will then be in the same position as you were, i.e. as to when the landlord may bring the tenancy to an end (see Chapter 4) and as to security (see Chapter 5). In particular, note that there is a mandatory ground for possession against an assured tenant who succeeds by inheritance.

But in addition to 'normal' rules of inheritance – and overriding them – special provision is made for inheritance – called 'succession' – to protected (including protected shorthold) and assured (including assured shorthold) tenancies (see Chapter 3). There are no such provisions for those with restricted contracts (see also Chapter 3). Bearing in mind that you may well be concerned with what has happened in the recent past, it is necessary to approach this subject under different headings.

A. Protected tenancies where tenant died before 15 January 1989

On the death of a protected tenant before 15 January 1989, either a spouse, or another member of his or her family could take over the tenancy. Only a spouse who was living in the premises at the time of death qualified – but if the spouse did qualify, he or she took precedence over any other member of the tenant's family.

One frequent problem is the 'common-law spouse', one person who has lived with another, as if they were married. Cohabitation is now quite common among the young, but the term 'common-law spouse' should be reserved for those who have been living together for many years, acting as if married, appearing to the 'outside world' as if married. Indeed, in one case, a man was held unable to qualify as 'common-law spouse' on the death of his partner, in part because the couple insisted on keeping and using their own names, since they wanted to avoid the appearance of marriage. (Of course, some couples actually married use their own names, but they will be spouses in law and qualify as such.)

There is no hard-and-fast rule: all the circumstances have to be taken into account – e.g. how long you had been together, how you liked to present yourselves to others, the nature of the relationship. The fact that one of the partners might in law have remained married to someone else, perhaps because they had never bothered to divorce or one of the spouses would not consent to divorce, should not prevent a finding of common-law marriage in the 'other' relationship.

If a legal spouse was living in the premises at the time of death, he or she takes precedence. A common-law spouse counts as a 'member of the family'. If there was no legal spouse to succeed, then another member of the family may have the tenancy. To qualify, the member of the family (including a common-law spouse) must have been living with the deceased tenant for at least six months before death. 'Living with' means living with as a home, not merely visiting occasionally (although it can be just one of two homes used by the relative – much in the same way as for statutory residence – see Chapter 5).

There may have been more than one qualifying member of the family. There could not be 'joint succession', so they must agree between themselves, or even apply to the court for a decision as to who should succeed. The choice is not the landlord's, and they do not even need to consult or inform the landlord, although of course it is polite and desirable to notify the landlord of the outcome of such a discussion or dispute.

There is, again, no fixed rule as to who qualifies as a 'member of the family' for these purposes: as well as common-law spouses, children, siblings, parents and grandparents, there are step-relationships, illegitimate relationships, in-law relationships, adoptive relationships and so on. There cannot, however, be the 'adoption' of one adult by another. On the other hand, adoption (of a child) may be a 'factual adoption' rather than one which happened formally or legally.

The successor took over the old tenancy. There could be up to two successions, so that a protected tenancy can go on for a long time, from parent to child to grandchild. Once both successions have been used up, however, the relatives (including spouse) of the 'third' tenant have no rights left in the property at all.

B. *Protected tenancies where the tenant died on or after 15 January 1989.*

The Housing Act 1988, which came into force on 15 January 1989, made a number of changes to the position as described under the last heading, which relate only to deaths on or after that date. In these cases, only a spouse can succeed to a protected tenancy, *as a protected tenant,* but where another member of the family succeeds he or she will get only *an assured tenancy.* However, for this purpose, where two people have been living together as man and wife without being lawfully married they are treated as spouses, rather than as members of the same family.

A member of the family will only qualify in the absence of a spouse (as thus defined) if he or she was living with the deceased tenant, in the property in question, and for a period of two years, rather than six months. However, if the death is within 18 months of 15 January 1989, for two years there is substituted a period of six months before that date, and continuously since it.

Furthermore, there will normally only be *one* succession. There can only now be a second succession – which will also be to an assured rather than a protected tenancy – where the would-be second successor was *both* a member of the family of the original tenant immediately before his or her death, *and* a member of the family of the first successor immediately before his or her death, and was residing with the first successor in the property in question, for two years before his or her death (with the same qualification for deaths within 18 months of 15 January 1989).

C. *Death of assured tenant.*
There can only be one succession to an assured tenancy, and only by a spouse, although this is also defined to include persons who have been living together as husband and wife. The succession is, of course, to an assured tenancy. There will be no succession unless the spouse was living in the property in question – although not necessarily with the deceased (they may have been separated) – immediately before his or her death.

There will be no succession if the tenancy was at some point in time a joint tenancy, and the deceased became the sole tenant on the death or departure of his or her other joint tenant(s). If the spouse is one of the joint tenants, there is no difficulty, because on the death he or she will himself or herself become the sole tenant. There will be no succession if the deceased tenant himself or herself became tenant under someone else's will or on his or her intestacy or under a *Rent Act* (protected tenancy) succession to an assured tenancy (above, *B*).

7: Rents in General

What rent do I have to pay?

The short answer is that you have to pay the rent which is part of your agreement, whether it is tenancy or licence. However, there are rent-control laws which apply in the case of protected and protected shorthold tenancies, restricted contracts and, to a much lesser extent, to assured and assured shorthold tenants (see Chapter 3). These laws are described in Chapter 8: the effect of the provisions means that in some cases, if you have one of these rights of occupation, you may not in fact have to pay the full rent that has been agreed. This will be considered in the next chapter. In this chapter, we are concerned only with the position which arises under the contract: as with security of tenure, it is necessary first to examine and understand the position under the contract, before turning to rights enacted by Parliament. The latter will, however, ultimately prevail, but they cannot be understood without understanding the contractual position first.

What is rent?

Rent is the name given to the amount you pay for your right of occupation. Unfortunately, it is sometimes used to mean different things. Thus, in some contracts 'rent' is used to mean a basic payment, to which may be added payments for what are called 'services' or the 'service charge' and for rates.

Do I have to pay rent in advance?

This depends on the terms of your agreement; protected and protected shorthold tenants cannot, however, be made to pay more than one period's rent, on the first day of the period – see Chapter 2.

What are rates?

Rates are payments required by the local authority, which depend on the rateable value of the premises you occupy: local authorities decide annually how much rates they will charge 'in the pound'. This means that they may decide to charge 50p in the pound, so that if you have a house with a rateable value of £300, your rates for that year will be £150. The authority can even charge more than one-for-one: they can decide to levy rates at an amount of, for example, £1.50 per pound, so that, in this example, the rates will be £450 for the year. Rates are to be abolished from 1 April 1990.

To whom will I pay my rates?

This will depend on your agreement. There are two broad possibilities: either you pay your rates to the local authority directly or you will pay them to your landlord, who passes them on to the authority. (He or she may even get a discount by taking this responsibility.)

Will my premises be separately rated?

If you are the tenant or the licensee of a whole house, your dwelling will almost certainly be separately rated. If you are the tenant or licensee of a self-contained flat, it is likely to be; if you are the tenant or licensee of a single room, or rooms in a flat which is not self-contained, it is unlikely to be separately rated.

How can I find out whether my premises are separately rated?

You can find this out by asking the local authority for your area.

What will it mean if my premises are not separately rated?

In this case, you will certainly be paying your rates to your landlord, because without separate rating there can be no separate or direct rate demand on you.

If my premises are not separately rated, will the rates be identified separately in the rent?

Almost certainly not. You will be paying a sum of money which is *inclusive* of rates, and you will only have anything to do with the 'rates element' in your rent if either you apply for housing benefit or the landlord is or claims to be entitled to pass on an increase in the rates without increasing the rest of your rent, either under the contract or under the rent-control laws if they apply to you (see Chapter 8).

If my premises are separately rated, will the rates be identified separately in the rent?

Probably. There is a number of different possibilities. For his or her own reasons, the landlord may have stated one rent, which is *inclusive* of rates, in which case the question of rates will come up in the same circumstances as described in the last answer. Secondly, your rent may be said to be exclusive of rates, and yet the landlord collects the rates, to pass them on to the local authority. In this case, the agreement will certainly permit the landlord to increase rates if the local authority puts the level up, and, again, they may be increased under the rent-control laws if they apply to you (see Chapter 8). Finally, you may be paying direct to the authority yourself, and in this case the rates are a matter between you and the authority, and the landlord has nothing to do with them: again, your rent is said to be *exclusive* of rates.

If I pay rates to the landlord, can he or she pass on increases to me?

This will depend on whether your rent is inclusive or exclusive, on what the agreement says and, where they apply to you, what the rent-control laws permit (see Chapter 8). If your rent is exclusive of rates, yet you pay them to your landlord, then (as noted in the last answer) the agreement will almost certainly permit him or her to pass on any increase. If you pay an inclusive rent, then if the agreement specifies that the rent can be increased on account of rates (which is relatively unusual) the landlord will be able to pass on the increase; otherwise, the position is governed by whether and how the landlord can increase the rent generally.

What are services?

Services are the activities involved in maintaining a house subdivided into flats or rooms, or a block of flats, which are common to all the rooms or flats, or which relate to the common parts (such as cleaning, lighting or heating of stairs, corridors, halls, bathrooms or lavatories). There may be a housekeeper or caretaker. In addition, heating (of space and hot water) may be provided to each of the rooms or flats. Then there is the management job itself, including such matters as insurance. Of particular importance is the function of maintaining and repairing the premises as a whole, or facilities such as a lift. On occasion, they may be payable in relation to a house, e.g. on an estate. I will refer here to flats, but the same remarks apply to houses.

What are service charges?

These are your share of the cost of services.

Will I have to pay a service charge in addition to the rent?

This depends on the contract. It would be exceptional for

a licence agreement to require this. It would also be exceptional for a tenancy of a single room, or of a flat which is not self-contained. It is more common in other flats.

Can the landlord increase the service charge?

If the agreement does not say that you have to pay a service charge separately from the rent generally, the landlord can only increase the service charge in the same circumstances and manner he or she can increase the rent (below). The main purpose of separating rent and service charge is in fact to permit the landlord to pass on increases, so that if the agreement identifies as part of your obligations payment of a service charge, it will almost certainly permit the landlord to pass on increases, and identify how and when he or she can do this. The rent-control laws, where they apply, may affect your obligations in this respect (see Chapter 8).

How much will I have to pay in service charges?

Normally, an agreement will specify an amount payable annually, which operates as a payment 'on account', i.e. you additionally have to pay any balance. The landlord cannot, however, charge whatever he or she wishes by way of service charge: the agreement will itself state for what services the charge is payable. Even then, service charges are limited by law (Landlord and Tenant Act 1985) to costs 'reasonably incurred', and only so far as works or services are carried out to a 'reasonable standard'. Where an amount has to be paid on account, or otherwise if the agreement permits the landlord to claim from you before works or services are carried out, the on-account sum is to be no more than a reasonable amount, and must make provision for repayment of an excess.

If the landlord wants to have work carried out on the building above a certain limit, he or she must also comply with controlling provisions. The limit is: £1,000, or £50 multiplied by the number of flats in the building, whichever is the greater. £1,000 is the limit, then, for a building in which there are twenty or fewer flats; £1,050 if twenty-one flats and so on.

The controlling provisions require the landlord to obtain at least two estimates for the work before it is carried out, and at least one of those estimates must be from a person or company with no connections with the landlord. Either the landlord has to display a notice of the works, accompanied by copies of the estimates, somewhere in the building where the notice is likely to come to your attention, or he or she must give you a copy. If there is a recognized tenants' association (see below), the association may be given these details and you will only be given 'summaries'. A tenants' association must also be given a detailed specification of the works, and you will get a summary. A tenants' association is allowed to make suggestions as to who is invited to give estimates.

The notice must describe the works to be carried out, and invite you to comment on those works, and on the estimates, and must provide a name and address in the United Kingdom to which, and a date by which, those observations may be sent. Your observations do not have to be, but clearly ought to be in writing, (and you ought to keep a copy). The date stated must be not less than a month after the notice and, unless the works are urgent, they must not be commenced before that date and before the landlord has taken your observations into account. If the service charge is later challenged in court, the court can ignore the landlord's failure to comply with any of these provisions if satisfied that the landlord acted reasonably.

You may wish to challenge the service charge because you think that it is more than you ought to pay, for instance because you do not believe that the costs have been incurred at all, or to the extent claimed, or that they are unreasonably high, or that the works are not to a reasonable standard, or that the landlord has failed to comply with any of the above provisions. (You may not agree, for example, that works were urgent enough to commence before the date specified in the notice accompanying estimates.) You can challenge the service charge by refusing to pay and defending the landlord's action against you for the money, or, preferably, by taking the initiative and seeking a ruling on the issue from the county court (which may include trying to reclaim money already paid to the landlord on account).

In order to decide whether or not you ought to challenge the amount, you are entitled to make a written request to the landlord, asking for a written summary of costs incurred during a particular period, and the landlord is obliged to answer within one month of your request, or six months of the end of the period in question, whichever is the later. (In effect, this recognizes that the landlord may have up to six months to prepare the accounts.) You can make this request through the secretary of the tenants' association, if there is a recognized one covering your home (see below). The costs cannot relate to works more than 18 months before the demand, unless notice was given during the 18 months after the works that the demand would later be forthcoming.

The summary has to set out the costs in a way which shows how they are or will be reflected in demands made to you for service charge payments. If there are more than four flats in your building, or if the costs cover works or services not only to your building but also to another building (for example, in the landlord's ownership or management), the costs have to be certified by an accountant, as a fair summary and adequately supported by accounts, receipts and other documents which the accountant has seen. You, either yourself or through the secretary of a recognized tenants' association, have the right in response to the summary to ask to see the full accounts, receipts or other documents, and to take copies of, or make extracts from, them. There is a number of other details which must be provided, including details of payments received by the landlord on account of service charges.

A recognized tenants' association is one which the landlord has agreed to recognize, by notice in writing given to the person you (the tenants) appoint as secretary. A landlord can withdraw recognition by prior written notice of at least six months.

Where they apply, the rent-control laws may affect or supplant these provisions: see Chapter 8.

How can the landlord increase the rent itself?

This, again, depends on the terms of the agreement. A periodic tenancy, or an indeterminate licence, will not usually say anything about how rent may be increased. Instead, if the landlord wants more rent, he or she can terminate your right of occupation by notice (see Chapter 4) and offer you a new tenancy or licence at a higher amount. Where the rent-control laws apply, this may not be possible (see Chapter 8). Where the rent-control laws do not apply, you will not have any security of tenure, and it follows that there is not much you can do about this.

It is for this reason that landlords often do not even have to bother bringing the agreement to an end and offering you a new one, because you are likely simply to *agree* a rent increase. It is really a straightforward choice between accepting rent increase or leaving – only if you have decided on the latter will it then be worth your while to force the landlord into bringing the tenancy or licence to an end properly, because you will only have to pay the former rent while your time runs out.

If there is a fixed-term agreement, this may make provision for 'rent reviews', i.e. increases, at specific times, and perhaps according to a specific formula (or, for example, by reference to some such concept as an 'open market' rent, perhaps to be decided by arbitration if you and the landlord do not agree). Unless there is provision for increases within the agreement, however, the landlord will not be able to increase your rent until the agreement runs out: this is one of the principal values of a fixed-term agreement, i.e. not just security for a stated period but at a stated amount. In either event, though, the rent-control laws where they apply may affect or overrule what has been agreed (see Chapter 8).

8: Controls on Rents

What controls are there on rents?

The controls on rents, apart from those afforded by your agreement (Chapter 7), are those which Parliament has applied to protected and protected shorthold tenants, assured and assured shorthold tenants and restricted contracts (see Chapter 3). Protected and protected shorthold tenants are able to take advantage of the 'fair rent' laws; there is provision for referring an assured tenant's rent to a rent assessment committee; restricted contracts may be made subject to Rent Tribunal rents.

What is a fair rent?

A fair rent is the amount which a Rent Officer has decided is the appropriate rent for premises, and has recorded in the register of fair rents. A Rent Officer is a government-appointed official. Fair rents apply *only* to protected and protected shorthold tenants.

When deciding what the fair rent for such a tenancy ought to be, the Rent Officer has to ignore two factors. First of all, he or she must ignore the fact that it is hard to find somewhere to live: this is known as disregarding the 'scarcity factor', and means that rents should not be higher because accommodation is scarce. Secondly, the Rent Officer has to disregard the 'personal circumstances' of either landlord or tenant, such as the wealth or poverty of either. For example, if a letting is of a flat on the top floor of a large house, and there is no lift, the fact that a lot of stairs have to be climbed to get to the flat will affect the rent. But it will affect rent equally whether you are young and sprightly or are elderly and find it difficult to climb stairs.

The Rent Officer will also take into account the terms of the tenancy (for example, whether or not there is use of a garden, who has to do what repairs) and the condition of the premises. The Rent Officer otherwise takes account of all the 'normal' factors which determine rents, such as location, nearby facilities (a park, a school, shops, transport and so on), and size and type of accommodation (house, flat, self-contained, with or without exclusive use of own toilet and bathroom).

One of the main ways in which the Rent Officer determines these questions is by use of 'comparables'. That is to say, he or she will examine the register of existing fair rents, to see what rents have been charged for similar property, in a similar locality. He or she will want to look at the more recent decisions, because these will obviously be the most relevant (because of inflation). Similarity of size, type of property, facilities and so on will be relevant. The comparable should then be adjusted for differences, such as inferior repair or other features, and time since it was registered.

When a fair rent is being fixed (see below), one or other of the parties may object to the decision of the Rent Officer. An appeal lies to a body known as the Rent Assessment Committee. If they decide a different fair rent, the Rent Officer enters it in the Rent Register, and it is the same as if the fair rent had been decided by the Rent Officer in the first place.

Will the fair rent include services?

It may do, or it may not. The landlord can ask the Rent Officer to fix a rent with a 'variable' service charge. This is only available to the landlord if the tenancy agreement is one under which you have to pay service charges which may vary from time to time according to the costs of services (see Chapter 7). The landlord will have to satisfy the Rent Officer that the method of calculating the service charge is itself reasonable, but this is not likely to be difficult to do in view of the controls on service charges described in the last chapter.

If the Rent Officer is *not* satisfied that it is right to permit a variable service charge, then in effect the cost of services has been taken into the main rent, and will only change when the rent changes (see below). However, if the amount which the Rent Officer believes is attributable to the cost of services is 5 per cent or more of the whole rent registered, he or she will make a note of the amount in the register.

If the Rent Officer permits a variable service charge, then rent will change in the way described below; and service charges will vary as described in the last chapter. Whether or not a variable service charge was permitted has to be taken into account when using other rents as comparables (see above).

Will the fair rent include rates?

No. Whether or not the tenancy agreement is inclusive of exclusive of rates (see Chapter 7), the amount registered as the fair rent will be exclusive. The exclusion of rates has to be taken into account when using other rents as comparables (see above).

Do fair rents apply to all protected and protected shorthold tenancies?

No. There is only a fair rent for a protected or a protected shorthold tenancy if one has been registered. This does not necessarily mean registered under your tenancy: it can have been registered in the past, when there may have been a different tenant, or even a different landlord. The rent is a rent for *premises*, not for *people*; by this I mean the fair rent is registered regardless of who the landlord is and who the tenant is. Once a fair rent is registered it remains the fair rent for the premises, *regardless* of whether tenant changes, or whether landlord changes, always provided of course, that the premises are still let on a protected or protected shorthold tenancy. There are only a few exceptions to this. If the fair rent was registered for an *unfurnished* letting, but a new letting is substantially *furnished*, then the registration is not applicable; it is wholly irrelevant and it is as if no fair rent was registered for those premises at all.

Also, the premises must be exactly the same. Thus, if the fair rent is for a letting of two rooms in a house, but the new letting is of three rooms, the fair rent which has been registered will be irrelevant. It will not work as the fair rent for two thirds, *plus* a figure for the third. It is an entirely new letting. In the same way, but perhaps less acceptably, if the fair rent was registered for three rooms, but your letting is of two, the fair rent is again irrelevant, and as if no fair rent had been registered – there won't be a registered rent of two thirds.

Once a fair rent has been registered, it remains the registered rent, indefinitely, until either the rent is re-registered, or the landlord applies for the rent to be removed from the register, in which case it is again as if no rent had ever been registered for the premises. The landlord can *only* do this: (a) two years or more after the last registration, and (b) at a time when there is no protected or protected shorthold tenancy of the premises.

Will there be a fair rent for my tenancy?
Yes, if either a fair rent was registered before your tenancy, is applicable and has not been removed (see last answer), or if you or the landlord apply to the Rent Officer to register a fair rent, which either of you may do at any time.

What is the effect of a fair rent registered before my tenancy began?
This may be discovered by inspecting the register (see

page 153). If a rent is already registered, and applies to your tenancy, this is the maximum which the landlord can charge, or ought to have been charging you. If you have been overcharged, you can claim the extra back from your landlord, or deduct it from future rent (although you should always give the landlord a choice, and always set out in writing what you are doing, with exact figures, and keep a copy of your letter). You can only claim back for up to two years' overcharging. Again, though, if you are paying a rent that is inclusive of rates (see Chapter 7), or if the rent registered is with a variable service charge (see above) and you are paying a rent that includes the service costs, you will have to allow for this before deciding if you have been overcharged.

How is a fair rent applied for?

Provided you are a protected or a protected shorthold tenant, either you or the landlord can apply for a fair rent to be fixed, at any time (unless one already exists, in which case the position is described in relation to re-registration, see page 161). Once one of you applies, the other will be notified. The application must be on the appropriate form, a copy of which is available from the local Rent Office, and from advice and aid agencies. If there are joint tenants, you should all sign the form, or if you do not all do so, those who sign should sign on behalf of all the joint tenants, and note on the form that they are doing so.

The form should be filled in as correctly as possible, and will require you to suggest what the fair rent ought to be. Use comparables (see page 154) to do this, by inspecting the register to see what other rents have been fixed. The register itself is maintained by the Rent Officer service, and is open for anyone to view. The address of the local Rent Office will be in the telephone directory, or available from an advice agency.

Both parties will be given an opportunity to tell the Rent Officer whether they want him or her to hold what is called a 'consultation', i.e. a hearing. It is usually advantageous for you to ask for a consultation in order to make sure that the Rent Officer is aware of all the defects in the premises, the drawbacks to living there, and also of answers to any points the landlord might make. Much might not be obvious unless pointed out by the person most experienced in the premises – the tenant.

It is important, therefore, when the Rent Officer writes asking if you want a consultation, to reply within the time stated in that letter. The Rent Officer will either himself or herself visit the premises, or arrange for a visit on his or her behalf. The Rent Officer might ask for further information, and this must be provided.

The hearing itself will usually take place at the Rent Office. It is an informal hearing, although parties may if they wish be represented, whether or not by a lawyer. There is no legal aid for these hearings, although a lawyer may be able to help with some of the preparatory work, for no fee or a small fee, (see Chapter 10). In some areas there is a Surveyor's Aid Scheme which may assist you: a local advice or aid agency will know whether there is one in your area, and how to get in touch with it.

If either landlord or tenant is dissatisfied with the decision of the Rent Officer, there is a right of appeal to the Rent Assessment Committee. Rent Assessment Committees have a reputation for *increasing* rents registered by Rent Officers, so that it is usually safer not to appeal. If the landlord appeals, however, you will wish to oppose any increase. If you do wish to appeal, the way to do so will be described in the letter from the Rent Officer which notifies you of his or her decision. It will state a time limit in which an appeal must be started, and it is important to comply with this limit.

The position as regards representation in front of the

Rent Assessment Committee, whether appealing or defending, is the same as before the Rent Officer (see above).

What is a certificate of fair rent?

If a landlord was intending to build or convert premises into new units, he or she might have sought a preliminary decision from a Rent Officer as to what the fair rent would be once the work was done. A landlord might have done this if there was no fair rent for existing premises, before deciding whether or not to grant a tenancy. The decision of the Rent Officer would have become the fair rent at a later date, provided conditions at time of registration were the same as those which it was said would be the case at the time of certificate.

In the case of a protected shorthold tenancy in Greater London (see Chapter 3), a landlord *must* have obtained such a certificate before the letting started, unless there was an actual fair rent in existence and applicable to the tenancy. Furthermore, he or she must, within twenty-eight days of the start of the protected shorthold tenancy, have applied for the certificate to be turned into an actual fair rent (and not subsequently withdrawn the application). In the period between start of tenancy and fixing of actual fair rent, the amount stated in the certificate is treated as having the same effect as if it had been actual – for example as to overcharging, or maximum rents,(see above).

What will be the effect of registration of a fair rent for my tenancy?

The fair rent is the maximum *rent* which the landlord can charge, and therefore which you have to pay. The main reason for applying for registration for a fair rent, therefore, is to secure a reduction in your rent, if you think it is too high. If you are in doubt, inspect the register for comparables (see above). If you are paying a rent which is inclusive of rates (see Chapter 7) or a potential comparable was registered with a variable service charge but you pay your service costs within your rent, remember to make the appropriate adjustments (see above).

When will the registration take effect?

If the rent registered is lower than your existing rent (allowing for rates if you pay an inclusive rent), the registration will take effect on the date the Rent Officer registers the fair rent. If there is an appeal, the Rent Officer's rent will apply until any new decision by the Rent Assessment Committee, and that will then apply from the date when the Committee tells the Rent Officer to enter the result in place of his or her decision.

If there is an increase in your existing rent, the position is more complicated. It is first necessary to ask whether you are a contractual or a statutory tenant (see Chapters 4 and 5). If you are a contractual tenant, the landlord cannot charge more than the contract permits (see Chapter 7).

If you have a periodic tenancy, the landlord can end the contractual tenancy by notice to quit. Alternatively, he or she can serve a notice of increase of rent, which will take effect as a notice to quit, if, but only if, the date stated in it, from when the increased rent is to start, is no earlier than the date on which the tenancy could have been brought to an end by notice to quit (i.e. usually four weeks or a month – see Chapter 4). In either case, he or she will not be able to gain the increase until after the contractual tenancy has ended, which will of course be later than the date of registration by the Rent Officer.

It may not be possible for the landlord to bring a fixed-term tenancy to an end, perhaps for a lengthy period. In the meantime, the landlord will not be able to pass the increase on, *unless* the agreement permits increases. Some modern agreements now specify in the alternative one amount, or whatever rent may be registered. This will permit the landlord to take advantage of the Rent Officer's increase. If there is no such provision in the agreement, the landlord will have to await the end of the term.

If the tenancy was already statutory at the time of registration, and the rent is increased, the landlord can claim the increase, from the date of registration, by notice of increase. The notice of increase can only be backdated, however, for up to six weeks, so that unless the landlord serves the notice within six weeks of date of registration, he or she will start to lose the benefit of the increase.

In all of these cases – contractual or statutory, periodic or fixed-term – the landlord cannot pass on the whole of the increase at once. The increase is subject to 'phasing', that is to say it is spread over two years. It is, however, only the 'strictly rent' element which is phased: rates can be increased in full (provided the agreement permits this), whether or not the rent is inclusive or exclusive of rates (see Chapter 7). The rent phasing works by allowing the landlord half the difference between the old rent and the new rent in the first year; and the full increased rent only in the second year. Service charges can also be increased in full.

Can a fair rent later be increased?

Yes, by re-registration. This can normally only happen after a two year gap. The landlord can apply for re-registration one year and nine months after the last registration, but the re-registration cannot take effect until the two year period has passed. There can also be an application for re-registration during the two years if there has been a significant change in circumstances relating to the rent, such as the introduction or removal of new furniture, a heating system, or serious damage to the property.

When a Rent Officer reconsiders a rent within the two-year period, for change of circumstances, he or she starts anew, rather than just considering the value of the change. This means that the possibility is rarely of use to you, because while you may be entitled to a reduction in rent for one reason, inflation will have increased it in other respects.

If the landlord and the tenant *agree* to do so, a joint application may be made in less than two years, but it is hard to think of circumstances when it would be in your interest to agree, for the same reason – that re-registration usually means an increase.

When will a later increase take effect?

The position is similar to increases when a rent is first registered: the increase cannot be passed on beyond the contractual rent limit without bringing the tenancy to an end, and the strictly rent element will be phased over two years. If the Rent Officer did not register a variable service charge on the earlier registration, but entered a 'service element' (i.e. 5 per cent or more of the rent – see page 155) the increase in the service element is not phased, in other words it may be passed on in full.

The increased rent is applicable from the date of its registration by Rent Officer (or, perhaps, twice: from initial registration by Rent Officer, and subsequent variation by Rent Assessment Committee – see above). If the tenancy is already statutory, the landlord must serve notice of increase, and can only backdate for up to six weeks. If the tenancy is still contractual, and periodic, it can be brought to an end either by notice to quit or notice of increase. If it is contractual and fixed-term, the landlord may not be able to take advantage of the increase at all.

It may be that the earlier registration reduced the rent to a level below the contractual rent. The landlord would not then necessarily have brought the contractual tenancy to an end. It may, of course, have run out (if fixed-term), or the landlord may have served a notice to quit for some other reason (including possibly to make you feel uncomfortable because you procured a rent reduction).

If the contractual tenancy continues, however, the rent under the agreement may *still* be higher than the amount the rent rises to on re-registration. In this case, the rent increase will be phased, but the landlord does not need to serve any notice of increase: that means the increase (to the phased level) is payable from the date of registration. Indeed, *part* of an increase may be recoverable in this way, without notice of increase, i.e. up to the contractual limit, so that the landlord might be entitled to some amount for a short period until he or she brings the contractual tenancy to an end, and then another amount once the tenancy becomes statutory.

The procedure on re-registration, including on appeal, is exactly the same as on a first or earlier registration.

Can the landlord increase my rent without registration?

If you are a protected or a protected shorthold tenant, the landlord must normally obtain a registration of fair rent before he or she can increase your rent, whether you are still a contractual tenant, or have become a statutory tenant (because a fixed-term tenancy has expired, or because the landlord has at some time served a notice to quit).

If you are still a contractual tenant, the position as regards increases for rates and services is described in Chapter 7. If your tenancy has become statutory, however, the landlord cannot increase for either rates or services without serving a notice of increase (which can be backdated for only up to six weeks). The landlord can use the notice of increase to turn a contractual, periodic tenancy into a statutory tenancy, in order to pass on rates or service increases, but only if the notice of increase states a date for the increase to take effect no earlier than the tenancy could have been brought to an end by notice to quit (i.e. usually four weeks or a month, see Chapter 4), and there can, therefore, in this case, be no back-dating.

The rent, then, is effectively frozen until there is a registration. There is an exception to this. The exception is if you and the landlord enter into what is called a 'rent agreement'. This is any agreement under which the two of you agree to a higher rent. It may take the form of an agreement varying your existing tenancy, or it may take the form of an agreement when the tenancy has already become statutory, or it may take the form of an offer of a wholly new tenancy. These are called rent agreements if the arrangement involves an increase, other than for rates, or other than one permitted by the original contract, such as for rates, service charges, or, indeed, a rent review (see Chapter 7).

A rent agreement is wholly invalid unless it is in writing, signed by both you and the landlord, and has a statement at the head of the document which contains certain information. The statement cannot be in 'small print'. Quite literally, the statement must be in print or writing 'no less conspicuous' than the rest of the document. The information must remind you that your security of tenure will not be jeopardized if you refuse to sign, that if you refuse to sign, and insist that the rent is registered, you will need to pay only half the increase in the first year ('phasing' – see above), and that even if the agreement is signed, either of you can still go to the Rent Officer at any time.

Although it is possible that a rent increase by agreement will be less than a rent set by the Rent Officer, you should be very sure that this is the case before agreeing.

Furthermore, because a rent set by the Rent Officer will be phased, with only half payable in the first year, the rent under an agreement has to be not only less than a registration would be, to be of any value to you, but at least 25 per cent less. (Rent agreement: increase from £500 per year to £1000 – two years = 2 × £500, = £1000. Registration: increase from £500 to £1000 – first year = £250, second year = £500, = £750. Therefore rent agreement must be from £500 to £875 to equal registration.)

It may be safely said that it is less commonly in your interests to enter into a rent agreement and, indeed, because of the technicalities, rarely that landlords even bother to use the procedure. If the landlord does not wish to go the Rent Officer, he or she may well try an 'informal agreement', i.e. one which does not comply with the technical requirements. An informal agreement is not binding on you, and any increase paid under it may be recovered, by deduction from rent or by legal action, as an over-payment, although only for one year back.

Do fair rents apply to assured tenants?
No. There is very limited control on the rent of an assured tenant. The position is different for assured tenants and assured shorthold tenants.

A. *Assured tenants.*
There is no rent control in respect of a fixed-term assured tenancy so long as it lasts: you will have agreed the rent for the term, or you will have agreed how the rent changes (e.g. by reference to inflation, or to arbitration). But when a fixed-term assured tenancy expires, it is followed by a periodic assured tenancy. At that time, either you or the landlord may seek to change the terms of the tenancy (other than rent), e.g. as to repairing obligations. If you do not agree the change, the matter can be

referred to the Rent Assessment Committee: that Committee can decide to change the rent to reflect some other change in the terms.

Otherwise, once your fixed-term asssured tenancy becomes periodic, you will be entitled to ask a Rent Assessment Committee to review the rent, *if, but only if,* the landlord seeks an increase. The same is true of an assured periodic tenancy which has always been so: the only control on rent is reference to the Rent Assessment Committee when the landlord seeks an increase. In the case of a periodic assured tenancy which has always been such, however, even this limited protection will not apply if the tenancy agreement itself contains a provision for fixing the rent – e.g. reference to arbitration, or increases or decreases in line with inflation or some other index.

The only control applies, therefore, and with the above-mentioned exceptions, when *the landlord* seeks an increase: you cannot enter, as a protected tenant can, into an agreement for a tenancy at a particular rent, and then go along to the Rent Officer for a lower rent to be fixed; nor if a lower rent was fixed for an earlier tenant is there anything to stop a landlord charging you a higher rent. You will have to pay what you have agreed unless and until the landlord seeks an increase.

An increase can only be sought by the landlord by serving a notice in the prescribed form, proposing a new rent to take effect at the beginning of a new period of the tenancy. The new period must itself be one beginning no earlier after service of the notice than one month in the case of weekly or monthly tenancies, six months in the case of a yearly tenancy or, in any other case, a single period (e.g. three months, six months) of the tenancy.

Furthermore, in the case of a tenancy which has always been periodic (rather than one which arose after a fixed term), the period from which the new rent is proposed cannot be any earlier than one year after the tenancy itself began. In addition, if the landlord has previously increased the rent in this way, the period from which the new rent is proposed cannot be any earlier than one year after the last increase took effect.

When the landlord has served the notice, then you as tenant can either accept it, or seek to agree a different increase, or apply to the Rent Assessment Committee to review the rent. But you have to make such an application, on the prescribed form (which will be available from most advice agencies, and from all offices of Rent Assessment Committees), *before* the period from which the new rent is proposed to take effect. This is very important: if the period from which the new rent is proposed has already started, you have lost your opportunity to refer the rent to the Committee until the next time the landlord seeks an increase.

There is a great danger, therefore, in allowing yourself to be drawn into negotiations by a landlord for so long that your right to refer the rent to the Committee is lost. If this seems possible, apply to the Committee in time, in any event, and if you and the landlord later reach your own agreement you can jointly write to the Committee withdrawing your reference, and the Committee will then be likely not to proceed with it. (It is entitled to do so, e.g. if it suspects that you have been pressured.)

If your application goes to the Committee, it will consider whether or not what the landlord has proposed is a reasonable open-market rent for an assured tenancy of your premises, on the terms on which you occupy them, subject to any notice which you may have been given relating to the mandatory grounds for possession (see Chapter 5). The Committee will *not* disregard 'scarcity', as in the case of a fair rent. The Committee will disregard the fact that you are already a sitting tenant, which customarily suggests a lower rent than otherwise.

The Committee will of course disregard any reduction

in the value of the property attributable to your failure to comply with your terms of tenancy, e.g. internal decoration, but it will also disregard any increase in value which is attributable to an improvement which you have carried out, or which was carried out in the previous twenty-one years by a former tenant, in each case provided that you were not or the former tenant was not obliged under the terms of your tenancy to carry out that improvement. A previous tenant's improvement is also only disregarded if the tenant did not quit, i.e. if you have succeeded to, inherited or had assigned to you the tenancy – see Chapter 6.

The rent which the Committee considers is exclusive of any service charge which can be tested under the Landlord and Tenant Act 1985: see Chapter 7. The Committee also considers rent exclusive of rates. The new rent will take effect from the beginning of the same period the landlord proposed, unless the Committee decides that this would cause undue hardship to you, in which case it may specify a later date (though no later than its decision). Until the Committee decision, however, there is no actual rent increase.

The provision for undue hardship reflects the fact that the Committee is unlikely to reach its decision for some months, perhaps long after the period when the landlord sought the increase from. You will therefore owe the landlord the difference, in effect backdated.

You should therefore save the difference between what you are paying, and what is proposed. But if you are on housing benefit, or unemployed, or in other difficulties, you may find this impossible, and these are the sorts of circumstances when undue hardship may be found. Always tell the Committee what efforts you have made to save the difference, or why you have been unable to save enough or anything, and why it would cause you undue hardship if the increase is effectively backdated.

If the increase is substantial, and the delay lengthy, you could even find that you owe more than three months' rent, in which case the landlord will be able to serve notice of seeking possession, and if you are unable to clear the balance before proceedings come to court a mandatory order could be made against you (see Chapter 5). This is an extreme, but powerful, illustration of undue hardship. The increase could cause your eviction!

There is no appeal against the Rent Assessment Committee's decision, although in a rare case it might be possible to review their decision because they have mis-understood or misapplied the law, or behaved so unreasonably that no Committee could property have reached its decision. Such an action is extremely difficult, and you will certainly need legal advice: see Chapter 10. There is, however, no legal aid available before the Committee, although some legal advice may be available, and the Surveyor's Aid Scheme referred to in connection with fair rents may be of assistance.

B. *Assured shorthold tenants.*

In the case of an assured shorthold tenant, if the landlord seeks an increase, the position is the same as in the case of an ordinary assured tenant. In addition, however, and so long as the shorthold is still within its original fixed term (see Chapters 3 and 4), the tenant can of his or her own accord refer the rent to the Rent Assessment Committee, on the grounds that it is excessive. This can only be done once: if the matter proceeds to a decision under this provision, there can be no second or further reference, and the tenant can only then await the landlord's next attempt to increase the rent (when the normal procedures apply).

'Excessive' means excessive compared to other assured tenancies, whether shorthold or not. But the Committee will not determine a rent for the tenancy unless it considers that there are sufficient other assured tenancies (whether or not shorthold) with which to compare. If the Committee determines a rent for the tenancy, it will only do so on the grounds that the rent payable under the assured shorthold is 'significantly higher' than might be expected otherwise.

The Committee will decide from when the new, *lower* rent will take effect, but it cannot be earlier than your application, so that if you decide to refer the rent in this way, it is best not to delay. If the Committee does set a lower rent in this way, that is all you are bound to pay. No increase can then be sought by the landlord for one year after the date from which the reduced rent takes effect. The rent considered by the Committee excludes service charges and rates, as in a normal case.

Do fair rents apply to restricted contracts?

No. However, there is an alternative system applicable to restricted contracts. Rents for restricted contracts may be determined by the Rent Tribunal. If you have a restricted contract, you should bear in mind the limitations on your security, both if you have a pre-Housing Act 1980 contract, and even more so if you have a post-1980 Act contract (see Chapter 5). In either event, application for a Rent Tribunal rent is likely to result in retaliatory eviction proceedings.

A tenant or licensee with a restricted contract only has to pay whatever rent is considered reasonable by the Rent Tribunal. Once a Rent Tribunal has registered a reasonable rent, that remains the rent for the premises in question, even if the registration was between a different tenant and/or landlord. However, the premises must be exactly the same – for example, the same number of rooms.

A landlord can apply for a rent by the Rent Tribunal to be removed from the register at any time more than two years since the last registration, provided that at the time he or she applies for removal from a register there is no restricted contract in existence. Otherwise, the registration remains effective indefinitely.

This means that if an occupier takes up a restricted contract and subsequently discovers that there was a rent registered with the Rent Tribunal which was lower, he or she has been overcharged and can recover the excess by legal action.

The provisions thus far are the same as those considered in relation to fair rents (see page 153). However, overcharged Rent Tribunal rent can be for up to six years' excess. In addition, it is a criminal offence for a landlord to overcharge on a restricted contract. This may be reported to the local authority's Tenancy Relations or Harassment Officer, who may consider prosecution.

The register of rents is maintained by the Rent Tribunal's employees. There is no 'officer' like the Rent Officer where restricted contracts are concerned: the initial decision is by the Tribunal, and there is no appeal as such. Anyone may inspect the register, and this is how to find out if there is an existing registration.

If there is an existing registration, this will be the limit that is payable, whatever the contract itself says. Registrations will be exclusive of rates, so that rates will have to be added. Services will not be noted separately. The nature of restricted contracts (see Chapter 3) is such that questions such as separate rates and service charges rarely come up. Since 1974 and until 15 January 1989 (when new restricted contracts ceased to be possible: see Chapter 3), restricted contracts had mainly been lettings by resident landlords.

If there is no existing registration, you, or the landlord, may apply to the Rent Tribunal for registration of a reasonable rent which, when registered, simply becomes the rent payable. Before registration, there will be a hearing at which both sides will be given an opportunity to make representations. The position as regards represent-ation and assistance is the same as for Rent Officer/Rent Assessment Committee hearings (see page 158).

If you have a pre-1980 Act contract (Chapter 5) and make an application for registration, and the landlord retaliates with notice to quit, the notice to quit is auto-matically deferred, at least until the rent hearing, and normally for up to six months thereafter unless the Rent Tribunal decides that a lesser period is appropriate (see Chapter 5). The same is true – for up to six months from the date of hearing – if the landlord serves a retaliatory notice following the Tribunal's decision.

Note, first of all, that this 'protection against retali-ation' only benefits you if you have a periodic tenancy or licence, because it operates by deferring notice, and notice is not given in connection with fixed-term agreements. Note, secondly, that the landlord can apply to the Tribu-nal or court for reduction of this automatic deferral (see Chapter 5). Finally, note that it is *only* applicable to pre-1980 Act contracts: post-1980 contracts enjoy no such protection at all.

Once there is a rent registered with the Rent Tribunal, a new application – which is likely to mean an increase and is therefore more likely to benefit the landlord than you – can only be made after two years, unless there has been a significant change in the condition of the dwelling, the furniture or the services provided, the terms of the contract, or some other factor taken into account when the last rent was registered. This, too, is as with fair rents (see page 161).

9: Repairs, Improvements and Alterations

REPAIRS

Who is responsible for repairs?

Mainly the landlord. If you are a licensee, the landlord will probably be liable for *all* repairs. The agreement may say otherwise. This may be because, for example, the licence is of short-life property scheduled for redevelopment, and it is of the essence of the agreement that you have been allowed in for a short time, in the present state of the premises, in effect *because* they are in such bad condition.

Normally, where a licence is involved, it is the landlord's responsibility to keep the premises in a condition fit for the purpose for which they were let, and as a rule of thumb this will be taken to mean in an internal condition approximating to that in which they appeared to be when let, and externally and structurally in a condition good enough to keep the premises in the same sort of state, i.e. wind and weathertight.

With two exceptions, under a tenancy, regardless of class of security (see Chapter 3), the landlord is responsible for all major repairs, *whatever the tenancy agreement says* (Landlord and Tenant Act 1985). The exceptions are: (a) tenancies for seven years or more; and (b) tenancies which began before 24 October 1961 (the date when the provisions came into force under the Housing Act 1961). A tenancy is a tenancy for seven years or more only if it is a fixed-term tenancy for that length of time: a periodic tenancy which has lasted, or may last, longer, will not qualify. In deciding whether or not the tenancy began before 24 October 1961, it is the original, contrac-

173

tual (see Chapters 4 and 5) tenancy which matters: this may be your own, or that of someone to whose tenancy you have succeeded (see Chapter 6). In these two cases, repairing responsibility will depend on the terms of the agreement; in the latter case (an 'old' but long-lived period tenancy), there may even be a 'gap' in responsibilities, although if the gap would make a nonsense of the tenancy (e.g. because though no one is responsible for *external* repairs, you are liable for *internal* repairs), the law may still *imply* a responsibility on the landlord.

For the purpose of this major repairing obligation where it applies (which will be in the vast majority of cases), major repairs means the structure and exterior of the property, and the installations for heating (both the premises, and water), and gas, electricity and water supplies, including basins, sinks, baths and lavatories. The landlord has to keep all of these elements of a property in proper repair and working order. The right does not extend to, for example, your own cooker, refrigerator or other installations.

Where you occupy a flat or room, 'structure and exterior' includes the outside walls of the flat or room, the floor, and the floor above the ceiling. In other words, the premises are defined as if they were not part of another building. The structure and exterior of the building itself are not structure and exterior of the flat or room. Similarly, facilities – e.g. a central heating boiler – in the common parts are not installations in the dwelling. In the case of tenancies beginning before 15 January 1989, therefore, the landlord's responsibility depends on *either* the contract itself, which may have so stated, *or* a term implied by law that the landlord would keep the common parts of a building with flats or rooms in it in acceptable condition, including, for example, not only halls, stairs, corridors and front door, but also the roof of the building. This would not apply to a house let as a whole.

In relation to tenancies beginning on or after 15 January 1989, and which (as above) are for less than seven years, however, the law now expressly states that the landlord is liable for the structure and exterior of a building in which a flat or room is situated, and for installations which directly or indirectly serve the flats or rooms. But this liability only arises if the defect affects your enjoyment or use of your part of the building.

These rights do not extend to internal decoration, or minor internal repairs. However, if the state of the interior is damaged – as it will be by, say, leaks or damp – because of the landlord's failure to keep the premises in repair, the landlord may have to put the interior back into proper condition. Similarly, if the interior condition is damaged (for example, wallpaper stripped off) to enable the landlord to carry out the repairs for which he or she is liable, the condition ought to be reinstated.

The rights do not cover damage done by the tenant, nor do they cover matters which you ought to keep in repair. You are under a general obligation to 'use premises in a tenant-like manner', that is to use premises reasonably, and normally, and to take reasonable care of them – for example, if going away for a long break to turn off water, electricity and gas as appropriate, cleaning windows, mending fuses, unblocking the sink, 'in short . . . the little jobs about the place which a reasonable tenant would do', as one judge put it. You are not, however, expected to do works to prevent 'normal wear and tear', i.e. the fact that property will deteriorate over time and with use. When 'wear and tear' becomes 'disrepair', the matter has become one for the landlord.

When deciding whether or not premises are in disrepair, you have to take into account the age, character and locality of the property. A new property may be expected to be, and to be kept, in better condition than an old property. There does come a point when a house is so old and rundown that it requires virtual renewal to be put back into acceptable condition; at that point, however, it is likely that the house will be so unfit that the local authority will have to take action (see below).

There are obvious problems which a landlord must attend to: leaking roofs and drains, broken or decayed brickwork, doors and windows broken or ill-fitting, plumbing not working and so on. The hardest question is whether the landlord is obliged to do anything about *rising* damp, which affects many old properties. In a new property, there either will or ought to be a damp-proof course or membrane; there may not be one in an older property. Whether or not the landlord has to do anything to prevent rising damp will depend both on extent, and on cost. One can ask: is the landlord being asked to turn an old house into a newly modernized one (not within an obligation to repair), or is the job small enough to be classed as a repair?

Landlords may not use neighbouring property in their own control in such a way as to damage the property they have let to you; nor, indeed, can any other neighbour. If works have been carried out to your premises, before or since you moved in, negligently, or in a less than work-manlike manner, any later defects are the responsibility of the landlord and/or the person carrying out the work.

Whose responsibility is it to find out about disrepair?

Yours, for the most part. If your premises are in disrepair, the landlord is not under an obligation to carry out the repairs until he or she has had notice of it. However, the notice need not come from you: it may be because a neighbour has complained (because of damage being done to his or her property), or because the local authority has told the landlord (see below). You do not have to tell the landlord in person; to tell an employee or agent will be sufficient. Furthermore, if a representative of the landlord is at the premises, and it can later be shown that he or she had noticed the disrepair (or, perhaps, a consequence of disrepair, such as serious and obvious damp stains from leaks, etc.), this will be enough 'notice'.

If you are concerned about disrepair in your home, you will do well to notify the landlord, in writing, and keep a copy of your letter. There can then be no argument about whether or not the landlord was 'on notice'. You should set out what is wrong as precisely as you can, although if you cannot say what the *cause* is you can simply describe the *effect*, e.g. 'The window won't open', 'The lavatory won't flush', 'The rain comes in', and so on.

In some cases, the landlord may be considered responsible for remedying disrepair even if you cannot show that notice has been given. This will be true of disrepair in the common parts, in neighbouring property in his or her control, and of disrepair caused by defective work he or she has had carried out. It may also be true if a court takes the view that the landlord *ought* to have known of the defect in your own premises, and to have done something about it (Defective Premises Act 1972). Obviously, though, the first step is still to ask the landlord to carry out the repairs needed.

Can the landlord enter the premises to inspect for disrepair or to carry out repairs?

Yes. You have to let the landlord in both to inspect and to carry out repairs. If you do not, you may have broken your tenancy or licence, and this may give rise to a ground for possession against a protected assured tenant (see Chapter 5), although in all probability this will only be used by the landlord as a means of getting a court to order you to let him or her (or, more probably, his or her work-people) in. Except in a case of emergency, however, the landlord ought to give at least twenty-four hours' notice of an impending visit, and the visit should be at a reasonable time.

If my landlord wants to repair, should I let him or her do so?

Generally, yes, although only if the works are really repairs, and not improvements or alterations (unless, of course, you are agreeable to the proposed improvements or alterations). You will not, for example, be able to claim damages or otherwise complain about lack of repair if the reason the landlord has been unable to do works is because you would not let him or her do so! Indeed, if you refuse, the landlord may well be able to get an order to force you to let the works be carried out, though if you do not have much security of tenure, the landlord's most likely response will be to bring your right of occupation to an end!

If you have enough security of tenure to be able to enforce your rights (for example, because you are a protected or assured tenant, or because you have some years to run on a fixed-term lease), you should try and ensure that exactly what is to be done, and how long it will take, is put in writing and signed by both of you. Thus, for example, if the landlord says that works will take three weeks, and will interfere with your use of the bathroom, but they then take ten weeks and interfere with your use of more of the house, you will have grounds for complaint, and damages, for the difference.

You should also seek compensation, probably by way of reduction in rent, for the period of disruption (having regard to both the length of time your home will be disrupted, and how much of it), as well, of course, as any damages to which you are entitled because of the disrepair *prior* to the works being carried out.

If your landlord wants to do works, you will do best to take advice as to all of these matters, and possibly have an adviser (see Chapter 10) to deal with the landlord on your behalf.

If my landlord asks me to move out for works to be done, should I agree?

You do not *have* to move out to let your landlord do works, *unless* the works can only reasonably be carried out with you out of occupation. In this case, as well as having the arrangement in writing, and covering your compensation, as in the last answer, you will need to make sure that there is agreement as to where you will stay while the works are being done, who will pay for alternative temporary accommodation, and who will pay for such other matters as storage of your belongings, electricity, etc., used by repair workers, and so on. Again, you should if possible have all these matters handled by an adviser (see Chapter 10). In the case of an assured or assured shorthold tenant, if you do not agree to move to allow the work to be carried out, this may allow the landlord to seek to evict you (see Chapter 5).

Two other points to watch out for. Make sure you have the agreement to return to occupation in writing: if the landlord later refuses to let you back in, you will be able to get a court order to get back in much more easily if you start off with the landlord's signed admission of your right to return. Secondly, be as exact as possible about the works which the the landlord is entitled to do: you do not want to come back and find that much more considerable works have been carried out, perhaps making it impossible for you to go on living there, for example because a bathroom has been installed in what was a bedroom!

If the landlord will not repair, is there anything I can do to make him or her do so?

Yes. One course of action is for you to take legal proceedings against him or her, to get an order to make him or her carry out the works that are necessary. Another course of action is to complain to the local authority, which has a range of powers with which to force landlords to do works. In addition, in two cases there is a right of direct complaint to a magistrate.

When can I take legal proceedings myself?

When any of the repairing obligations described above have been broken by the landlord, you will be entitled to use the civil courts (see Chapter 10) to obtain an order to carry out the works, *and* for monetary compensation for any loss you have suffered as a result of the landlord's failure. This may be compensation for direct loss (such as damaged property, or clothing), or for less direct loss, such as additional heating costs, or eating out because facilities are not working, or even staying elsewhere because the premises became uninhabitable, or it may be for less easily quantifiable loss, such as for ill-health or reduced enjoyment of the premises.

However, you must bear in mind that in most cases the landlord's duty to repair will not start until he or she has been put on notice (see above), and, if the duty to repair has not commenced, there will be no breach of duty – in which case, the landlord will not be responsible for loss caused. (He or she will still have to carry out the repairs, because you will invariably have given forewarning before starting court proceedings and notice will accordingly, necessarily, have been given.) This limitation on the landlord's liability will not apply where the damage is in the common parts, or in neighbouring premises under his or her control, or results from negligent or defective work to your premises, or where a court takes the view that the landlord ought to have known about and repaired the defect (see above). Where there is a number of flats in disrepair, and the landlord will not do the repairs, it may, in an extreme case, be possible to get a court order for someone to take over the house or blocks and 'manage' (including repair) it instead of the landlord (Landlord and Tenant Act 1987): you will certainly need qualified legal help to do this (Chapter 10).

Can I withhold rent to make the landlord do the repairs?

Theoretically, yes; in practice, this is an extremely dangerous tactic. It is dangerous because if, at the end of the day, for this reason or that (want of notice, not landlord's responsibility, not bad enough disrepair, etc.), you are shown to be wrong, you will be in rent arrears. While this should not cause an outright order for possession against a protected tenant (see Chapter 5), it may none the less worsen your position. In the case of an assured tenant on the other hand, if the arrears are sufficient, they could result in an outright order for possession (see Chapter 5). Most other classes of occupier have such little security of tenure that this tactic runs a high risk of retaliatory eviction.

The law permits you to withhold rent in order to pay for works of repair which are the landlord's responsibility, and even to compensate yourself for losses you can claim from the landlord. Most major repairs, however, will cost far more than you will be able to pay out of the rent, however long it is accumulated, and there is an obvious risk that you will be more generous in compensating yourself for losses than a court would be.

Where you do decide to run the risk of withholding rent and having works carried out yourself (for example, if they are relatively minor), you should always give the landlord (a) an opportunity to do the work himself or herself, (b) a warning of your intentions, (c) a copy of estimates (you should obtain at least two estimates, preferably three), and (d) the choice of reimbursing you directly or having the money stopped from the rent. Each such warning or notification to the landlord should be in writing, you should always keep a copy of the letter and you should at each stage permit the landlord a reasonable opportunity to reply, or put the works in hand.

When can the local authority force my landlord to repair?

Local authorities have a range of powers to take proceedings to force landlords to repair. Some of these proceedings involve criminal prosecutions of the landlord, others do not. The authority may take proceedings against a landlord where there is what is known as a 'statutory nuisance' (Public Health Act 1936). This means *either* that the premises are in such a state that there is a risk to your health, or that of any other occupant, or that there is a defect in common parts or neighbouring premises under the landlord's control, which is causing harm to your premises.

The local authority also has powers under the Public Health Act 1936 in relation to: insufficient numbers of lavatories, or lavatories in an unsatisfactory state; insufficient food storage space; vermin (although its powers are wide enough to make *you* rather than the landlord cure this defect, though it will almost certainly only do this if the presence of vermin is your fault); and common lodging-houses.

Under the Housing Acts, the authority has powers related to unfitness for human habitation, serious disrepair (designed to prevent premises becoming unfit for human habitation), conditions such as might interfere with your personal comfort (such as dangerous wiring, dampness enough to be prejudicial to your health, or to qualify the premises as unfit for human habitation), and houses in multiple occupation. These Housing Act powers, and the Public Health Act powers described above, are cumulative, that is to say that they can all be used if necessary, although an authority will normally select and use one only first; if that fails, it may try another power.

The unfitness provisions are the principal powers used by authorities, not least because if they find that premises *are* unfit for human habitation, they *have* to take action. The action depends on whether the premises can be made fit at a reasonable expense or not. If they can, the authority serves a repairs notice; if they cannot, the authority takes action which will normally lead to an agreement or an order not to use the premises for human habitation any longer. Such an order will result in a protected or protected shorthold, or assured or assured shorthold tenancy ceasing to be protected or assured for the purposes of security of tenure (see Chapter 5).

In the case of such a 'closing order or agreement' you will always be rehoused by the authority (unless you are a trespasser), *and* normally compensated for having to move (unless a trespasser). How much compensation will depend on (a) your class of security, and (b) length of time in occupation – you should get a minimum of the reasonable costs of moving, but may get a cash payment as well if you are a tenant or a licensee under a restricted contract or in tied accommodation, and have been such for five years before action is taken.

Unfitness means that the premises are *so* defective in relation to one or more of the following matters that they are not reasonably suitable for occupation in that condition: repairs; stability; freedom from damp; internal arrangement (such as steep or insecure stairs, bathroom or toilet leading off from kitchen or living-room, sudden changes in floor level); natural lighting; ventilation; water supply; drainage and sanitary conveniences; and, facilities for preparing and cooking food and for disposing of waste water. Or, where a flat or room is involved, unfitness can be because of the condition of the building as a whole.

It follows that a major defect in one respect could lead to a finding of unfitness, or that several minor defects could do so. In one case, the only window in one of the bedrooms of a small house had a broken sashcord. It could only be opened at the risk of injury. This meant that the house could not properly be ventilated. The judge said: 'If the state of repair of a house is such that by ordinary user [use] damage may naturally be caused to the occupier, either in respect of personal injury to life or limb, or injury to health, then the house is not in all respects fit for human habitation'. This does not mean, of course, that *every* broken sashcord will make *every* house unfit for human habitation, simply that something as small and apparently as trivial or as easy to repair *may* have that effect.

If the proceedings lead to a closing order or agreement, it will be an offence for you to continue to occupy the premises, and the authority may even take possession proceedings itself. In practice, nothing is usually done until a proper offer of rehousing has been made, and time given to accept it.

The provisions governing houses in multiple occupation are even greater than those available for houses or flats. A house in multiple occupation (HMO) is a house which is occupied by people who do not make up a single household, such as different families, or different tenants under different tenancies, or a hostel. A women's refuge has been held to be an HMO; so has a hostel for alcoholics and the mentally disturbed; so has a house in which people had single rooms, but shared a kitchen; the most common form, indeed, is a house of bedsitting rooms.

Local authorities have power to issue directions, limiting the number of people who can live in an HMO. They can direct how many people can live in a particular room or part of an HMO. They may introduce 'registration schemes', which require owners of HMOs to register their properties, or particular classes of HMO properties, so as to enable them to keep a general record of how much housing in their areas is in multiple occupation.

In addition, an authority may serve a works notice on the owner of an HMO, in order to make the premises reasonably suitable for the number of people or households actually living in the property, in relation to: means of escape from fire; natural and artificial lighting; ventilation; water supplies; personal washing facilities; drainage and sanitary conveniences; facilities for storing, preparing and cooking food, for disposal of waste water; and for space heating.

The authority can order that part of a house should not be used, if this will mean that the rest of the house is inadequately served with means of escape from fire: this is effectively a closing order (or agreement) like that described above, with the same consequences as to loss of protection if a protected or protected shorthold or assured or assured shorthold tenancy, and rehousing and compensation.

In houses with at least three storeys on and above ground level (i.e. excluding basements – which includes basements not fully below ground level, but only mainly below ground level), of which the combined floor area (including stairs and corridors and other common parts) is more than 500 square metres, local authorities are under a *duty* to ensure that adequate means of escape from fire have been provided.

These powers may not, however, be enough. Mere repair, or even fire safety, may not bring about adequate living conditions. Local authorities have two more powers which they may be urged to use by an occupier in an HMO for the benefits of the occupiers of the property generally.

The first such power is the 'management order'. If it seems to the authority that an HMO is in an unsatisfactory state because of a failure to maintain proper standards of management, it may order that the 'management regulations' shall apply to the property. This means that the landlord has to obey a series of regulations, and standards, specified by the government.

The management regulations concern such matters as: repair; clean condition of house; good order and continuity of water supplies and drainage; repair, good order and continuity of gas and electric supplies; lighting, heating and hot water in the common parts (shared facilities); repair of rooms when let out anew, and for their maintenance in good repair; repair and good order of windows and other means of ventilation; repair, good order and freedom from obstruction of means of escape from fire; display of fire escape notices; keeping the garden (if any) tidy; general precautions to protect occupiers from injury; and provision for litter and refuse.

The final special power available to local authorities in relation to houses in multiple occupation, is that of the 'control order'. This is an order under the terms of which, quite literally, the local authority takes over the property as a whole, and manages it itself. It is also bound under a control order to draw up and execute a scheme of works designed to put the HMO into a good state of repair and order, and to maintain decent standards.

The control order may be imposed in one of four circumstances: when a works notice has been served; when overcrowding directions have been given; when the management regulations have been imposed; or whenever it appears that, although the authority has not taken action under any of these provisions, conditions in the HMO are such that it *could* take such action. In effect, it may bypass these stages and move direct to the control order.

Under whichever set of circumstances applies, however, the power is only exercisable when it appears to the authority that living conditions in the HMO are such that it is necessary to make the order for the protection of the safety, welfare or health of people living in the property. The inclusion of 'welfare' means that an authority could use the power if there is a fear of, for example, wholesale evictions, or harassment.

The control order provisions are very quick to operate. They are deliberately immediate, so as to prevent evasive action by a landlord, or retaliation against occupiers generally, or perhaps an individual occupier who has complained to the authority and caused it to use its power. From the date of the order, the authorities are in the position of landlords, for so long as the order lasts, i.e., they take full charge, and collect the rents. The order will normally last for five years, unless the landlord successfully appeals against it.

The authority can even grant new rights of occupation (although not fixed-term tenancies). This is an important part of the powers, because where the occupants have held on, for instance, licences (Chapter 1), or their tenancies are under an arrangement which deprives them of protection (see Chapters 1, 3 and 5), the authority can substitute a new, and proper, tenancy agreement.

Can I force the authority to take action?

You can only force the local authority to take action against your landlord if the authority is under a *duty* to do so, as distinct from when it merely has *power* to do so. Even when there is a duty, it is extremely difficult to force authorities to take action, because so often it is a mere matter of *opinion* whether or not their duty has arisen – for example, whether or not there is a statutory nuisance, or premises are actually unfit.

In either case, (duty or power), you can complain to the Local Ombudsman about the inaction of your authority. This should be done by asking your local councillor to forward your complaint, but if he or she will not do so, you can still ask the Local Ombudsman to look into the matter. The Local Ombudsman cannot actually order the authority to do anything, but can make a finding of maladministration, i.e. that the authority has not behaved as properly as it ought. Such a finding usually results in corrective action by the authority.

When can I complain to a magistrate?

You can go direct to a magistrate about statutory nuisance, or about unfitness. If you go about statutory nuisance, you are in effect prosecuting the proceedings against the landlord yourself (see further Chapter 10, as to why this may be a difficult undertaking). If you complain about unfitness and the magistrate agrees that your home is unfit for human habitation, he or she will direct the matter to the local authority's attention. Although you may already have been to the authority without success, this will prompt it (though not require it) to look further into the matter, and report back to the magistrate, if only as a matter of courtesy to him or her. This procedure will not amount to a prosecution of your landlord.

IMPROVEMENTS AND ALTERATIONS

Do I have the right to carry out improvements to my home?

Only protected tenants (Chapter 3) have a 'right to improve' their own dwellings, not protected shorthold tenants, and not even protected tenants if they have been given a notice that one of the mandatory grounds for eviction may apply, such as returning owner-occupier, retirement home, letting by person in the services – see Chapter 5. Otherwise, you will only have such a right if your agreement says so.

For the purpose of the statutory entitlement, an improvement includes addition or alteration to a dwelling, putting up an external television or radio aerial, and external decorations. The written consent of the landlord must be obtained, but the landlord cannot refuse consent unreasonably, i.e. for no reason at all, whimsically, or out of stubbornness.

If a landlord refuses consent, he or she must give a statement of reasons, also in writing. You may challenge your landlord's refusal of consent, by issuing proceedings in a county court for a declaration by a judge that the refusal was unreasonable, and that you may therefore go ahead.

Among the reasons which will be considered acceptable are that the 'improvement' would make the dwelling less safe or would make neighbouring premises less safe, or because it would mean the landlord has to incur extra expenditure (for example, on works to an estate which will be more difficult and costly because of the alteration), or because the improvement would mean that, if you quit, the landlord will get less rent for the premises or a lower price on a sale.

You should think very carefully before deciding to improve, whether under the agreement or under the statutory right. While your rent will probably not increase on account of the works you carry out, your rates may do so, and in any event you will be spending money on a property that is not ultimately your own and that you may not be able to stay in for ever (if, for example, you fall on hard times and suffer eviction for arrears, the landlord will not be obliged to compensate you).

An improvement grant *may* be available from the local authority. Be warned, though, that improvement grants are deceptive entities. You cannot get an improvement grant to do whatever you want: if you apply, the local authority decides what *must* be done in order to qualify for grant-aid *at all.* This produces a schedule of works, and a resulting cost. The improvement grant, however, will not be for this full cost, but to a government-specified limit, which is often much lower than the cost of the schedule specified by the local authority. Even then, it is still not the amount specified by the government which is paid, but an 'appropriate proportion' of that amount, which may be as little as 50 per cent, and only occasionally rises to 90 per cent, and even less frequently to the full 100 per cent.

Can my landlord be forced to carry out improvements?

In some circumstances, yes. There are two circumstances in which a local authority may compel a landlord actually to *improve* standards in a property, going beyond mere repair, or the prevention of unfitness (see above). Improvement for these purposes means the provision of 'standard amenities' and may apply when one or more of them are absent: fixed bath or shower; wash-hand basin; sink; hot and cold water supply at each bath, shower, wash-hand basin or sink; and, a water closet (WC).

Where there is a house or building with more than one dwelling in it – i.e. flats – these should be present in each dwelling; the WC ought to be inside the dwelling; the bath or shower ought to be in a bathroom, but if this is not possible, can be fixed in another room, other than a bedroom (for example, a kitchen). In addition, a programme of improvements should result in a dwelling in good repair, fit for human habitation, properly insulated, and likely to remain in an acceptable condition for fifteen years. The authority can, however, waive some of the specific requirements if it thinks the standard is too high (for example, by not requiring separate WCs inside each dwelling).

Improvement notices can only be served in relation to

older housing, i.e. built or converted into flats before October 1961. Notices can be served by the local authority, on its own initiative, in areas known as Housing Action Areas, and General Improvement Areas, which are areas selected and declared by the authority for general renewal or improvement. They are usually in the inner cities. Notices can be served outside these areas, only if the authority is asked to do so by an 'occupying tenant' (which means any class of tenant, but only a licensee if the licence is a restricted contract – see Chapter 3).

Because the works are extensive, you may have to move out while they are carried out. The authority will not pursue the procedure until housing arrangements have been made for you. This means that there has to be a *written* agreement between you, landlord and local authority, setting out where you are to live during the works, and what is to happen when the works are completed, i.e. your right to return. The arrangements may also cover care of your furniture.

If the works will take a long time, or you are elderly or infirm and ought not to have to move more than once, 'arrangements' may lead to permanent rehousing by the authority. This will not happen unless you want it to.

Can my landlord carry out improvements against my wishes?

Unless there is provision for this in your agreement, then the landlord can only do this without bringing your tenancy to an end and evicting you if (a) you are a protected or protected shorthold tenant, and (b) he or she has a court's permission. In deciding whether or not to make such an order, the court will take account of your age and health, accommodation arrangements during works, and inconvenience. These provisions only apply where the works are themselves the subject of an improvement grant application to, and likely to be approved by, the local authority.

A landlord under such a power, may, however, try to improve or alter beyond the class of works which fall within the improvement-grant system – for example, to convert a house not in self-contained flats into such flats (which are saleable), or to try to add another flat. Such works will be inconvenient and disturbing while carried on, and *may* alter your own premises. The landlord will not be able to do this without either evicting you, or gaining your agreement. You will have to weigh up the effect on you (which, of course, could mean betterment of your own living conditions), the extent to which you wish to remain in the same premises (as opposed to a permanent or temporary move elsewhere), the disturbance, and the extent of your own security, i.e. if you do *not* agree the landlord may be able to evict you (even if you are a protected or protected shorthold tenant, he or she may be able to obtain an order on the basis of an offer of alternative accommodation). Always make sure you make all arrangements (both for during works, and after, including your right to return if you are to be temporarily moved) in writing, and keep a copy of the agreement.

In the case of an assured or assured shorthold tenancy, the landlord may be able to evict you in order to carry out improvements: see Chapter 5.

10: Legal Proceedings, Advice and Assistance

Where will legal proceedings take place?
Legal proceedings can take place in a number of places. Legal proceedings, strictly so-called, are always in a court. This may be a civil court or a criminal court. The civil court will usually be the county court, but may be the High Court. It will normally be the High Court if included in your case against your landlord is a claim for compensation of more than £5,000 (whatever the claim is for – harassment, eviction, disrepair – *except* a claim for overpaid rent or illegal key money, and *some* classes of action for illegal eviction, which can be in the county court regardless of value). A criminal case will always *start* in the magistrate's court, but may go to the Crown Court for the full trial. In addition, proceedings may be heard in a Rent Tribunal or Rent Assessment Committee.

Do all legal proceedings take a long time to be heard?
No. A *full* case may well take a long time – many months, or even years. In cases of urgency, however, the *civil* courts have power to hold an immediate – interim – hearing, to decide what state of affairs should prevail until the full trial. This can even be a one-sided hearing, i.e. you can present your case and the court can make a short-term order for a few days or a week until it can hear your landlord as well, and then decide how things should stand until trial. There can be several such interim hearings if there are changes before trial. These interim hearings are extremely useful in cases of harassment or eviction, and also if there is serious and urgent disrepair. The criminal courts have no such interim powers.

Can I get legal aid?

You can get proper legal aid to bring or defend a civil case, but only to defend a criminal case. It is for this reason that I have given few details in this book about your right to prosecute your landlord for some of the many offences he or she may commit in relation to your tenancy. To give you enough advice to enable you to prosecute on your own would require very much more space than this book allows: see *The Lawyer–Client Handbook* in this series. That means you would have to use the services of a lawyer to prosecute. (This is not so in the case of a complaint of unfitness to a magistrate, but probably is so even in the case of a complaint of a statutory nuisance: see Chapter 9. In the latter case, however, there are several advice and aid agencies with sufficient experience to help you prosecute: they will not charge for their services – see further below.)

In a civil case, before a court, legal aid is means-tested. Means-testing is carried out on behalf of the legal aid authorities by the Department of Social Security. This will mean an appointment additional to those you have to keep with your lawyer: always try to keep this appointment or you may lose your right to legal aid.

Some lawyers are not keen on legal-aid work (while others do little else). You would do well to consult an advice or aid agency about which laywers you can expect to give you a friendly reception if you are proceeding under legal aid. This is useful for another reason: because traditionally not many lawyers have specialized in legal aid work, they may not be very experienced at it. Checking with an advice or aid agency increase your chances of finding a lawyer competent in this type of work.

Legal aid exists to cover your legal costs, including such related costs as, for example, those of a surveyor in a repairs case. You may qualify for legal aid with a 'nil contribution', in which case the whole of your legal costs will be met; or you may not qualify because of your income; or you may qualify, but subject to a contribution towards your costs.

If you are on a nil contribution, and you lose your case, you will normally not have to pay anything to the other side. If you have to pay a contribution to your own costs, and lose, you may have to pay an equal amount to the other side.

If you win, the other side should pay your costs, but be warned that this may be on a lower rate than your own lawyer is entitled to charge, so there could end up a balance to be met out of legal aid (and, in turn, that may mean that part of your contribution is still payable). If you win on legal aid, and the landlord has to pay you any compensation, the legal aid authorities are entitled to recoup out of that sum any money they have had to pay – for instance, because you are on a nil contribution, and the landlord's payment of your costs is not payment in full.

There is no full legal aid (but see 'legal advice', page 196) for proceedings before a Rent Officer, Tribunal or Assessment Committee.

Can I conduct a case myself?
I have already remarked that to conduct a criminal case yourself would be so difficult that, with no legal aid available, I have hardly bothered to refer to the possibility at all. It is also true that it is difficult to conduct your own case in the civil courts, and if legal aid is available it is preferable to use the services of a lawyer.

You do not have to use a lawyer, however. It is easier to conduct your own case if you are defending (for example, a possession action) than if you are bringing the action (such as for overpaid rent, or disrepair), but you are more likely to be at risk of losing your home in an action you have to defend, than in one you bring to court yourself.

It is not possible in a book of this length to describe how to bring or defend legal proceedings, although in the case of a small claim, you will be able to get advice from court officials, and if you are defending an action you will, similarly, get some help, either from court officials, or indeed from the judge (part of whose duty it is to ensure that people do not suffer from the want of a lawyer).

As a general rule, you should be careful to comply with any instructions which accompany forms from a court: for example, if a possession claim is issued against you, you ought to indicate within two weeks whether or not you propose to defend, and on what grounds. You are unlikely, as a litigant in person, to be penalized for non-compliance with such requirements, but you will certainly be better placed if you do.

Always attend a court at the time and place stated on a court form: there is nothing more disastrous than failure to turn up. If you *cannot* do so, perhaps because you are ill, *always* notify the court in advance, and in writing, and if possible send someone along to explain to the judge (not just to a court official). Do *not* leave the explanation until later, when orders against you may have been made and you have to try to get them set aside.

Appearances before the Rent Tribunal, Officer or Assessment Committee, are actually *intended* to be informal, and to operate with unrepresented people (although you are entitled to be represented by a lawyer if you wish, and can afford one). It is still necessary, however, to comply with directions on forms sent to you, and to attend when and where instructed.

Can I get help with legal advice?
In addition to the legal aid scheme, there is a legal advice scheme which enables a lawyer to administer a rough-and-ready means-test, and give you advice (including

letter writing, and filling in forms, but falling short of actually appearing on your behalf before a court), either for free or for a small sum of money. This is particularly useful in relation to the Rent Tribunal or Rent Officer or Assessment Committee, or if you are trying to prosecute a criminal case yourself, when full legal aid is not available.

In addition, there is now a number of advice and aid agencies which operate either through voluntary or government funding and which as a rule make no charge for their services, which can extend to full representation. The best known of these are the Citizens' Advice Bureaux which have, over the years, built up a considerable experience in advising tenants. There is likely to be one in or near your area. CAB do not usually undertake representation in court, but can in other forums.

There are also Law Centres, of which the staffs include qualified, practising lawyers, who will frequently appear in court, either to defend or bring a case, and in housing matters either in the civil or the criminal courts. They will also act in other forums. There may be a Law Centre in your area. They may utilize legal aid (in order to increase the otherwise inadequate funding of these agencies), but will rarely ask for money from you. Always co-operate with their efforts to get you covered by legal aid: they are helping you, and by your co-operation you can help them to help others.

In addition, the majority of local authorities maintain Housing Aid Centres. These have the advantage that, if you are entitled to accommodation from the authority themselves, you are in effect 'in touch' with them from the outset of your problem; their disadvantage is that, for this same reason, they may be more inclined to advise you to defend what is perhaps not a defensible action. There is also a number of other local advice and action agencies, most of which will help in housing matters.

Finally, there are specialist agencies, only a few of

which employ their own practising lawyers, but who will usually be fairly well experienced in housing matters. The central such specialist agency is in London: SHAC, the Housing Aid Centre, 189a Old Brompton Road, London SW5 (telephone: 01-373 7276).

The names of local agencies, or sometimes of solicitors appropriate for this sort of work, can be obtained from the Legal Action Group, 242 Pentonville Road, London N1 9UN (telephone: 01–833 2931), and from Shelter, 88 Old Street, London EC1 (telephone: 01–253 0202). Shelter maintains local groups covering a number of areas and will be able to tell you if there is one in your area.

It will always be worthwhile to contact a local advice or aid agency before approaching a solicitor, for the reason stated above: they will be able to put you in touch with lawyers willing to work on legal aid, and possibly with the necessary experience. To make contact with the local Government Ombudsman, when you wish to complain of local government action or inaction (see Chapter 9), write to: Commission for Local Administration in England, 21 Queen Anne's Gate, London SW1 (telephone: 01-222 5622), and Commission for Local Administration in Wales, Derwen House, Court Road, Bridgend, Mid-Glamorgan, CF31 1BN (telephone: 0656–61325).